Contents

KU-767-686

A guide to KET

The KET examination is part of a group of examinations developed by Cambridge ESOL called the Cambridge Main Suite. The Main Suite consists of five examinations which have similar characteristics but are designed for different levels of English language ability. Within the five levels, KET is at Level A2 (Waystage) in the *Council of Europe's Common European Framework of Reference for Languages: Learning, Teaching, Assessment*. It has been accredited in the UK as an Entry Level 2 ESOL certificate in the National Qualifications Framework.

Examination	Council of Europe Framework Level	UK National Qualifications Framework Level
CPE Certificate of Proficiency in English	C2	3
CAE Certificate in Advanced English	C1	2
FCE First Certificate in English	B2	1
PET Preliminary English Test	B1	Entry 3
KET Key English Test	A2	Entry 2

KET is a popular exam with candidates who are learning English out of personal interest and for those who are studying for employment reasons. It is also useful preparation for higher level exams, such as PET (Preliminary English Test) and other Cambridge ESOL examinations.

KET is an excellent first step, helping you to build your confidence in English and measure your progress. If you can deal with everyday basic written and spoken communication (for example: read simple articles, understand signs and notices, write simple notes and emails), then this is the exam for you.

There are two versions of KET available: KET and KET for Schools. KET for Schools was introduced to meet the needs of the increasing number of younger candidates taking KET. Both KET and KET for Schools follow exactly the same format and the task types, testing focuses and level of the question papers are identical. The only difference in the two versions of the exams is that the content and treatment of topics in KET for Schools are particularly targeted at the interests and experience of younger people.

Cambridge
Key English Test
5

WITH ANSWERS

Examination papers from
University of Cambridge
ESOL Examinations

CAMBRIDGE
UNIVERSITY PRESS

CAMBRIDGE UNIVERSITY PRESS
Cambridge, New York, Melbourne, Madrid, Cape Town, Singapore, São Paulo, Delhi, Dubai, Tokyo

Cambridge University Press
The Edinburgh Building, Cambridge CB2 8RU, UK

www.cambridge.org
Information on this title: www.cambridge.org/9780521123075

First published 2010

Printed in the United Kingdom at the University Press, Cambridge

A catalogue record for this book is available from the British Library

ISBN 978-0-521-123051 Student's Book without answers
ISBN 978-0-521-123075 Student's Book with answers
ISBN 978-0-521-123105 Audio CD
ISBN 978-0-521-123136 Self-study Pack

Topics

These are the topics used in the KET exam:

Clothes
Daily life
Entertainment and media
Food and drink
Health, medicine and exercise
Hobbies and leisure
House and home
Language

People
Personal feelings, opinions
  and experiences
Personal identification
Places and buildings
School and study
Services

Shopping
Social interaction
The natural world
Transport
Travel and holidays
Weather
Work and jobs

KET content: an overview

Paper	Name	Timing	Content	Test focus
Paper 1	Reading/ Writing	1 hour 10 minutes	Nine parts: Five parts (Parts 1–5) test a range of reading skills with a variety of texts, ranging from very short notices to longer continuous texts. Parts 6–9 concentrate on testing basic writing skills.	Assessment of candidates' ability to understand the meaning of written English at word, phrase, sentence, paragraph and whole text level. Assessment of candidates' ability to produce simple written English, ranging from one-word answers to short pieces of continuous text.
Paper 2	Listening	30 minutes (including 8 minutes transfer time)	Five parts, ranging from short exchanges to longer dialogues and monologues.	Assessment of candidates' ability to understand dialogues and monologues in both informal and neutral settings on a range of everyday topics.
Paper 3	Speaking	8–10 minutes per pair of candidates	Two parts: In Part 1, candidates interact with an examiner. In Part 2, they interact with another candidate.	Assessment of candidates' ability to answer and ask questions about themselves and about factual, non-personal information.

Paper 1   Reading and Writing

Paper format

The Reading section contains five parts. The Writing section contains four parts.

Number of questions

There is a total of 56 questions: 35 in Reading and 21 in Writing.

Sources

Authentic and adapted-authentic real-world notices, newspaper and magazine articles, simplified encyclopaedia entries.

Answering

Candidates indicate answers either by shading lozenges (Reading) or by writing answers (Writing) on an answer sheet.

Timing

1 hour 10 minutes.

Marks

Each item carries one mark, except for question 56 (Part 9), which is marked out of 5. This gives a total of 60 marks, which is weighted to a final mark out of 50. This represents 50% of the total marks for the whole examination.

Preparing for the Reading section

To prepare for the Reading section, you should read the type of English used in everyday life; for example, short newspaper and magazine articles, advertisements, tourist brochures, instructions and recipes, etc. It is also a good idea to practise reading short communicative messages, including notes, emails and cards. Remember, you won't always need to understand every word to be able to do a task in the exam.

Before the exam, think about the time you need to do each part and check you know how to record your answers on the answer sheet (see page 146).

Part	Task type and format	Task focus	Number of questions
1	Matching. Matching five prompt sentences to eight notices, plus an example.	Gist understanding of real-world notices. Reading for main message.	5
2	Three-option multiple choice. Five sentences (plus an integrated example) with connecting link of topic or story line.	Reading and identifying appropriate lexical item.	5

3	Three-option multiple choice. Five discrete three-option multiple-choice items (plus an example) focusing on verbal exchange patterns. **AND** Matching. Five matching items (plus an example) in a continuous dialogue, selecting from eight possible responses.	Functional language. Reading and identifying the appropriate response.	10
4	Right/Wrong/Doesn't say **OR** Three-option multiple choice. One long text or three short texts adapted from authentic newspaper or magazine articles. Seven three-option multiple-choice items or Right/Wrong/Doesn't say items, plus an example.	Reading for detailed understanding and main idea(s).	7
5	Multiple-choice cloze. A text adapted from an original source, for example encyclopaedia entries, newspaper and magazine articles. Eight three-option multiple-choice items, plus an integrated example.	Reading and identifying appropriate structural words (auxiliary verbs, modal verbs, determiners, pronouns, prepositions, conjunctions, etc.).	8

Preparing for the Writing section

To prepare for the Writing section, you should take the opportunity to write short messages in real-life situations, for example to your teacher or other students. These can include invitations, arrangements for meetings, apologies for missing a class, or notices about lost property. They can be handwritten or sent as email.

Before the exam, think about the time you need to do each part and check you know how to record your answers on the answer sheet (see page 147).

Part	Task type and format	Task focus	Number of questions
6	Word completion. Five dictionary definition type sentences (plus one integrated example). Five words to identify and spell.	Reading and identifying appropriate lexical item, and spelling.	5
7	Open cloze. Text type that candidates can be expected to write, for example a short letter or email. Ten spaces to fill with one word (plus an integrated example) which must be spelled correctly.	Reading and identifying appropriate words, with a focus on structure and/or lexis.	10
8	Information transfer. Two short authentic texts (emails, adverts, etc.) to prompt completion of another text (form, note, etc.). Five spaces to fill with one or more words or numbers (plus an integrated example).	Reading and writing appropriate words or numbers, with a focus on content and accuracy.	5
9	Guided writing. Either a short input text or rubric to prompt a written response. Three messages to communicate in writing.	Writing a short message, note or postcard of 25–35 words.	1

Part 6

This part is about vocabulary. You have to produce words and spell them correctly. The words will all be linked to the same topic, for example jobs or food. You have to read a definition for each one and complete the word. The first letter of each word is given to help you.

Part 7

This part is about grammar and vocabulary. You have to complete a short, gapped text of the type you could be expected to write, such as a note and reply, or a short letter. You must spell all the missing words correctly.

Part 8

This part tests both reading and writing. You have to use the information in two short texts (for example a note, email or advertisement) to complete a document such as a form, notice, diary entry, etc. You will need to understand the vocabulary used on forms, for example *surname, date of birth*, etc. You will need to write only words or phrases in your answers, but you must spell correctly.

Part 9

You have to write a short message (25–35 words). You are told who you are writing to and why, and you must include three content points. To gain top marks, all three points must be included in your answer, so it is important to read the question carefully and plan what you are going to write. Before the exam, practise writing answers of the correct length. You will lose marks for writing fewer than 25 words, and it is not a good idea to write answers that are too long.

Mark Scheme for Part 9

There are five marks for Part 9. Minor grammatical and spelling mistakes are acceptable, but to get five marks you must write a clear message and include all three content points.

Mark	Criteria	
5	All three parts of the message clearly communicated. Only minor spelling errors or occasional grammatical errors.	
4	All three parts of the message communicated. Some non-impeding errors in spelling and grammar or some awkwardness of expression.	
3	All three parts of the message attempted. Expression requires interpretation by the reader and contains impeding errors in spelling and grammar.	Two parts of the message clearly communicated. Only minor spelling errors or occasional grammatical errors.
2	Only two parts of the message communicated. Some errors in spelling and grammar. The errors in expression may require patience and interpretation by the reader and impede communication.	
1	Only one part of the message communicated.	
0	Question unattempted, or totally incomprehensible response.	

Paper 2   Listening

Paper format
This paper contains five parts.

Number of questions
25

Task types
Matching, multiple choice, gap-fill.

Sources
All texts are based on authentic situations, and each part is heard twice.

Answering
Candidates indicate answers either by shading lozenges (Parts 1–3) or by writing answers (Parts 4 and 5) on an answer sheet.

Timing
About 30 minutes, including 8 minutes to transfer answers.

Marks
Each item carries one mark. This gives a total of 25 marks, which represents 25% of the total marks for the examination.

Preparing for the Listening test

The best preparation for the Listening test is to listen to authentic spoken English for your level. Apart from in class, other sources of English include films, TV, DVDs, songs, the internet, English clubs, and other speakers of English, such as tourists, guides, friends and family.

   You will hear the instructions for each task on the recording and see them on the exam paper. There are pauses in the recording to give you time to look at the questions and to write your answers. You should write your answers on the exam paper as you listen. You will have eight minutes at the end of the test to transfer your answers to the answer sheet (see page 148). Make sure you know how to do this and that you check your answers carefully.

Part	Task type and format	Task focus	Number of questions
1	Three-option multiple choice. Short, neutral or informal dialogues. Five discrete three-option multiple-choice items with visuals (plus an example).	Listening to identify key information (times, prices, days of week, numbers, etc.).	5
2	Matching. Longer informal dialogue. Five items (plus an integrated example) and eight options.	Listening to identify key information.	5
3	Three-option multiple choice. Longer informal or neutral dialogue. Five three-option multiple-choice items (plus an integrated example).	Taking the 'role' of one of the speakers and listening to identify key information.	5
4	Gap-fill. Longer neutral or informal dialogue. Five gaps to fill with one or more words or numbers (plus an integrated example). Recognisable spelling is accepted, except with very high-frequency words (e.g. *bus*, *red*) or if spelling is dictated.	Listening and writing down information (including spelling of names, places, etc. as dictated on recording).	5
5	Gap-fill. Longer neutral or informal monologue. Five gaps to fill with one or more words or numbers (plus an integrated example). Recognisable spelling is accepted, except with very high-frequency words (e.g. *bus*, *red*) or if spelling is dictated.	Listening and writing down information (including spelling of names, places, etc. as dictated on recording).	5

Paper 3 Speaking

Paper format

The paper contains two parts. The standard format for Paper 3 is two candidates and two examiners. One examiner acts only as an assessor and does not join in the conversation. The other examiner is called the interlocutor and manages the interaction by asking questions and setting up the tasks (see Paper 3 frames on pages 102–113).

Task types

Short exchanges with the interlocutor and an interactive task involving both candidates.

Timing

8–10 minutes per pair of candidates.

Marks

Candidates are assessed on their performance throughout the test. There are a total of 25 marks, making 25% of the total score for the whole examination.

Preparing for the Speaking test

Take every opportunity to practise your English with as many people as possible. Asking and answering questions in simple role plays provides useful practice. These role plays should focus on everyday language and situations, and involve questions

Part	Task type and format	Task focus	Timing
1	Each candidate interacts with the interlocutor. The interlocutor asks the candidates questions. The interlocutor follows an interlocutor frame to guide the conversation, ensure standardi-sation and control level of input.	Language normally associated with meeting people for the first time, giving information of a factual, personal kind. Bio-data type questions to respond to.	5–6 minutes
2	Candidates interact with each other. The interlocutor sets up the activity using a standardised rubric. Candidates ask and answer questions using prompt material.	Factual information of a non-personal kind related to daily life.	3–4 minutes

about daily activities and familiar experiences. It is also a good idea to practise exchanging information in role plays about things such as costs and opening times of, for example, a local sports centre.

Assessment

You are assessed on your own individual performance and not in relation to the other candidate. Both examiners assess you: the assessor awards marks according to Grammar and Vocabulary, Pronunciation, and Interactive Communication; the interlocutor awards a mark for overall performance.

Grammar and Vocabulary

This refers to your ability to use vocabulary and structure. It also covers the ability to paraphrase to convey meaning.

Pronunciation

This refers to the intelligibility of speech. Having an accent from your first language is not penalised if it does not affect communication.

Interactive Communication

This refers to your ability to take part in the interaction appropriately. Hesitation while you search for language is expected and is not penalised so long as it does not strain the patience of the listener. Candidates are given credit for being able to ask for repetition or clarification if necessary.

Further information

The information in this practice book is designed to give an overview of KET. For a full description of all of the Cambridge Main Suite exams, including information about task types, testing focus and preparation, please see the relevant handbooks which can be obtained from Cambridge ESOL at the address below or from the website: www.CambridgeESOL.org.

University of Cambridge
ESOL Examinations
1 Hills Road
Cambridge
CB1 2EU
United Kingdom

Telephone: +44 1223 553355
Fax: +44 1223 460278
Email: ESOLHelpdesk@Cambridgeassessment.org.uk

Test 1

PAPER 1   READING AND WRITING (1 hour 10 minutes)

PART 1

QUESTIONS 1–5

Which notice (A–H) says this (1–5)?
For questions 1–5, mark the correct letter A–H on your answer sheet.

Example:

0   You must use this door between these hours.

Answer:

	0	A	B	C	D	E	F	G	H
		☐	☐	☐	☐	☐	☐	☐	■

---

1   Young people and their parents may choose different meals. E

A   FIRE EXIT ONLY – NO ENTRANCE TO GARDEN

B   Bed and Breakfast Only £24.95

2   You can eat here in the evenings. D

C   This way to the restaurant garden ⇒

3   The waitress will show you where to sit. G

D   Dinner is served in the restaurant until 10.00 p.m. daily

4   You can stay the night here. B

E   There is a special children's menu – please ask your waitress

F   **Galaxy Restaurant** *We have high chairs for young children*

5   You should not usually use this door to go outside. A

G   RIVERSIDE RESTAURANT Please ask us to find you a table

H   *Antec Computers* All staff must use night entrance 8 p.m. – 6 a.m.

PART 2

QUESTIONS 6–10

Read the sentences about working in a library.
Choose the best word (A, B or C) for each space.
For questions 6–10, mark A, B or C on your answer sheet.

Example:

0   Elena .... a Saturday job working in a library a few months ago.

    A   got   **B**   became   **C**   was   *Answer:*   **0**   A ■   B ☐   C ☐

---

6   On Saturdays, a lot of people visit the library where Elena works and it is always ......A........ .

    A   busy   **B**   heavy   **C**   strong

7   'The job is ......B........ because I meet a lot of different people,' Elena says.

    A   friendly   **B**   interesting   **C**   favourite

8   Her job is to .... all the books when people bring them back.

    A   look   **B**   watch   **(C)**   check

9   Elena has to put all the books back on the .... shelf.

    A   good   **B**   possible   **(C)**   right

10   Sometimes people ......B........ to return their books on time.

    A   think   **(B)**   forget   **C**   mind

PART 3

QUESTIONS 11–15

Complete the five conversations.
For questions 11–15, mark A, B or C on your answer sheet.

Example:

0

Where do you
come from?

A New York.

B School.

C Home.

Answer: 0 A B C
■ □ □

---

11 Have a good holiday.

A Thanks, I will.

B I think so.

C Yes, very much.

12 What about going shopping this afternoon?

A I'm too tired!

B What a pity!

C That's not right!

13 I can't do my homework.

A Can you be careful?

B You can't have that.

C Of course you can.

14 Which of the boys is your friend?

A He says I'm right.

B Yes he is, isn't he?

C That one over there.

15 I've waited here for two hours!

A Yes you do.

B I'm sorry about that.

C It didn't matter.

QUESTIONS 16–20

Complete the conversation about a game of tennis.
What does Juan say to Rob?
For questions 16–20, mark the correct letter A–H on your answer sheet.

Example:

Rob: Are you free on Saturday afternoon?

Juan: **0** ....**D**................

Answer: | **0** | A B C D E F G H |

Rob: Would you like to play tennis?

Juan: **16** ....C.................

Rob: Yes, at the sports centre at 3 o'clock.

Juan: **17** ....F.............

Rob: That's OK. You'll be fine!

Juan: **18** ....H...............

Rob: About an hour should be enough.
We can stop if we get tired.

Juan: **19** ....E.............

Rob: Your house is nearer to the sports
centre so I'll see you there at 2.30.
We can go in my car.

Juan: **20** ....B..............

Rob: No problem. It'll be fun.

A Are you a good player?

B Great! Then we won't have to walk back. Thanks very much.

C OK. Have you booked somewhere to play?

D Yes. I'm not doing anything.

E Alright. Where shall I meet you?

F You know I haven't played for a long time.

G It's not expensive to play.

H How long are we going to play for?

PART 4

QUESTIONS 21–27

Read the article about two Canadian boys.
Are sentences 21–27 'Right' (A) or 'Wrong' (B)?
If there is not enough information to answer 'Right' (A) or 'Wrong' (B), choose
'Doesn't say' (C).
For questions 21–27, mark A, B or C on your answer sheet.

A great idea!

Frazer and Peter are two 14-year-old boys who grew up in the same small Canadian town. They have always been friends and classmates. Like all their other friends, they enjoy going fishing or swimming at weekends. But for the last few months, they've spent every weekend in Peter's room working on his laptop. This isn't because they have a lot of homework. They have made a new computer word game.

The idea for the game came from Frazer's little brother, Kevin, who had problems with his reading. Kevin learns words more easily by seeing pictures and hearing information than he does by reading. His brother wanted to help. Frazer and Peter worked together for over 200 hours to make a computer game and now it's ready to use. It's a speaking and picture game. For example, if you look at the word 'hat', there's a drawing of a hat next to it and you can hear Peter saying 'Hat! Hat!' at the same time.

The two boys have won a lot of prizes for their computer game and it will soon be on sale around the world. Many schools are interested in buying it.

Example:

0   Peter and Frazer are both teenagers.

    A   Right   **B**   Wrong   **C**   Doesn't say   *Answer:* | **0** | A B C ■ □ □ |

---

21   Peter and Frazer go to the same school in Canada.

    (**A**)   Right   **B**   Wrong   **C**   Doesn't say

22   Peter and Frazer like doing different sports to their friends.

    A   Right   (**B**)   Wrong   **C**   Doesn't say

23   For the past few months, the boys have spent most of their time outside.

    A   Right   (**B**)   Wrong   **C**   Doesn't say

24   Peter and Frazer prefer playing computer games to doing their homework.

    A   Right   **B**   Wrong   (**C**)   Doesn't say

25   It took less than 200 hours to finish the new computer game.

    A   Right   (**B**)   Wrong   **C**   Doesn't say

26   In the computer game, you see a picture of a word and hear it spoken.

    (**A**)   Right   **B**   Wrong   **C**   Doesn't say

27   Students in other countries have said they would like to use the computer game.

    A   Right   **B**   Wrong   (**C**)   Doesn't say

PART 5

QUESTIONS 28–35

Read the article about parrots.
Choose the best word (A, B or C) for each space.
For questions 28–35, mark A, B or C on your answer sheet.

Parrots

Perhaps you have seen **(0)** .... beautiful birds, with their lovely colours and long tails in the forest or in the zoo. Parrots are **(28)** .....C....... in countries like Brazil, Australia and India. They usually live in large groups and **(29)** ......C...... they like to eat fruit, they are **(30)** ......B...... a problem for farmers.

(31) .....C...... are many different kinds of parrots, but they all have strong beaks and feet, which they use **(32)** ......A...... climbing and holding food. The biggest birds **(33)** ......A..... live for up to 80 years.

They are **(34)** ......B...... noisy, but they are clever birds and it is easy to teach them to talk. Some zoos have parrot shows, where you can see the birds **(35)** ......B...... things they have learned.

Example:

0	**A** this	**B** these	**C** them	*Answer:*	0

28	**A** finds	**B** find	**C** found

29	**A** so	**B** that	**C** because

Lee

30	**A** somewhere	**B** sometimes	**C** something

31	**A** Here	**B** They	**C** There

32	**A** for	**B** by	**C** with

33	**A** can	**B** did	**C** are

34	**A** more	**B** very	**C** much

35	**A** done	**B** doing	**C** does

PART 6

QUESTIONS 36–40

Read the descriptions of some things you need to enjoy different hobbies.
What is the word for each one?
The first letter is already there. There is one space for each other letter in the word.
For questions 36–40, write the words on your answer sheet.

Example:

0   If you enjoy taking pictures, you'll need one of these.   c __ __ __ __ __

Answer:

0	c a m e r a

---

36   If you enjoy camping, you'll need this to sleep in.   t E N T

37   People learn to play music on this.   g u i T A R

38   If you like reading stories about pop stars, you may
need to buy these every week.   m A G A Z S N E S

39   People who like walking in the forest need these to
keep their feet dry.   b O O T S

40   If you enjoy watching films at home, you may
need to rent this.   v i D E O

PART 7

QUESTIONS 41–50

Complete the email from Greg to his friend, Anna.

Write **ONE** word for each space.

For questions 41–50, write the words on your answer sheet.

Example: | **0** | *n o t* |

| **From:** | Greg |
| **To:** | Anna |

Hi Anna,

I'm **(0)** .... having a very good week!

Yesterday my team had **(41)** ....a.......volleyball match, but we lost. The other team played much better **(42)** ....THan. we did! Then my friend Jeff, who lives in Australia, telephoned with bad news. He can't come to stay **(43)** ...Witth... us during the holidays because he's got a summer job. We can't **(44)** .....go...... camping together now. And this morning, my sister got **(45)** .....up.... late so she rode my bike **(46)** .....To... school! She didn't tell **(47)** ....me.. she needed to use **(48)** .....it..... . I'm really angry with **(49)** .....HER.

I hope you have some good news! Write back today **(50)** ....IF...... you can.

Greg

PART 8

QUESTIONS 51–55

Read the advertisement and the note about a theatre centre.

Fill in the information in Sarika's notes.

For questions 51–55, write the information on your answer sheet.

ANGEL THEATRE CENTRE

Saturday, June 22nd and
Sunday, June 23rd

Large Theatre – *The Last Man*
Small Theatre – *Storm*

Saturday	2 pm
	5 pm
Sunday	11 am
	1 pm

Adult £10.00   Students £6.00

Dear Sarika,

Do you know my cousin? She has just started at our university.

She wants to come to the theatre with us. Both days are fine, but I would like to go in the morning.

I've heard that *The Last Man* is boring so perhaps we should see the other play. Thanks for booking this.

Sarika's notes

Trip to: Angel Theatre Centre

Name of play:	**51**	Storm
Time:	**52**	11 AM
Date:	**53**	23 June
Number of people:	**54**	3
Price per person:	**55**	£ 6

PART 9

QUESTION 56

Read this email from your friend, Mike.

From:	Mike
To:	Ma—

So you finally bought a mobile phone. Tell me about it. What do you like about it? How much did it cost? What colour is it?

Write soon.

Write an email to Mike and answer his questions.
Write 25–35 words.
Write the email on your answer sheet.

PAPER 2 LISTENING (approximately 30 minutes including 8 minutes transfer time)

PART 1

QUESTIONS 1–5

You will hear five short conversations.

You will hear each conversation twice.

There is one question for each conversation.

For questions 1–5, put a tick (✔) under the right answer.

Example:

0 How many people were at the meeting?

3	13	30
A ☐	B ☐	C ✔

---

1 How will Jill go to the football match?

A ☐   B ☐   C ☐

2 Who's going to visit the woman?

A ☐   B ☐   C ☐

3 What will Ruby do tonight?

A ☐

B ☐

C ☐

4 How much did the woman's <u>desk cost</u>?

A ☐

B ☐

C ☐

5 Where is the man's watch?

A ☐

B ☐

C ☐

PART 2

QUESTIONS 6–10

Listen to Lena talking to a friend about some restaurants.
What is the problem with each one?
For questions 6–10, write a letter A–H next to each restaurant.
You will hear the conversation twice.

Example:

0   Rose Garden   **B**

Restaurants

6   Carla's Café   ☐

7   Pizza Place   ☐

8   Curry House   ☐

9   Captain Crab   ☐

10   Carlton Hotel   ☐

Problems

A   closed

B   cold

C   dark

D   expensive

E   full

F   noisy

G   small

H   unfriendly

PART 3

QUESTIONS 11–15

Listen to Helen talking to her friend, Sam, about being in a rock band.
For questions 11–15, tick (✔) A, B or C.
You will hear the conversation twice.

Example:

0   In Nick's band, Helen

    A   plays the guitar.   ☐

    B   sings.   ✔

    C   plays the drums.   ☐

---

11   Sam agrees to play the guitar on

    A   Wednesday.   ☐

    B   Thursday.   ☐

    C   Friday.   ☐

12   Where does Nick's band practise?

    A   in a garage   ☐

    B   at Helen's flat   ☐

    C   in Nick's bedroom   ☐

13   Sam should bring

    A   sandwiches.   ☐

    B   CDs.   ☐

    C   a sweater.   ☐

14   The band will next play at

    A   a party. ☐

    B   a club. ☐

    C   a college. ☑

15   How much does Helen earn, <u>per night, in the band</u>?

    A   £10 ☑

    B   £25 ☐

    C   £110 ☐

PART 4

QUESTIONS 16–20

You will hear a man talking on the telephone about a party.
Listen and complete questions 16–20.
You will hear the conversation twice.

Party for old school friends

For pupils from:	Romford School
Date of party:	**16** .... September
Day of party:	**17**
Place:	Margaret's house
Margaret's new surname:	**18**
Margaret's address:	**19** 11 .... Road
Bring:	**20**

PART 5

QUESTIONS 21–25

You will hear some information about a place called Sea World.

Listen and complete questions 21–25.

You will hear the information twice.

Sea World

Open: Tuesday–Sunday

Closed during <u>month of</u>:   **21** _____

Watch a film about the sea in: **22** The _____ Centre

Dolphin show starts at: **23** _____ p.m.

Shop <u>sells</u>:   **24** _____ and books

Child's ticket costs: **25** £ _____

You now have 8 minutes to write your answers on the answer sheet.

PAPER 3   SPEAKING (8–10 minutes)

The Speaking test lasts 8 to 10 minutes. You will take the test with another candidate. There are two examiners, but only one of them will talk to you. The examiner will ask you questions and ask you to talk to the other candidate.

Part 1 (5–6 minutes)

The examiner will ask you and your partner some questions. These questions will be about your daily life, past experience and future plans. For example, you may have to speak about your school, job, hobbies or home town.

Part 2 (3–4 minutes)

You and your partner will speak to each other. You will ask and answer questions. The examiner will give you a card with some information on it. The examiner will give your partner a card with some words on it. Your partner will use the words on the card to ask you questions about the information you have. Then you will change roles.

Test 2

PAPER 1   READING AND WRITING (1 hour 10 minutes)

PART 1

QUESTIONS 1–5

Which notice (A–H) says this (1–5)?
For questions 1–5, mark the correct letter A–H on your answer sheet.

Example:

0   This is not a good place to leave your bags.   *Answer:*

		A	B	C	D	E	F	G	H
0		☐	☐	☐	☐	☐	☐	■	☐

---

1   You must have a ticket to go past here.

> **A**   These ticket machines take £20 and £10 No credit cards

2   If you want to travel Monday to Friday, this ticket is cheaper.

> **B**   These seats are for people with heavy suitcases

> **C**   Sorry – restaurant is closed on today's London–Glasgow train

3   Please let anybody carrying a lot of luggage sit here.

> **D**   Passengers only through this gate Have your ticket ready

4   You can only buy your ticket here if you have cash.

> **E**   Station Café open all day (opposite ticket office)

> **F**   Passengers with bicycles pay £5 extra on this train

5   People who are travelling can eat something here.

> **G**   Please do not leave luggage here

> **H**   Save money: buy a weekly travel ticket here

PART 2

QUESTIONS 6–10

Read the sentences about a lake.
Choose the best word (A, B or C) for each space.
For questions 6–10, mark A, B or C on your answer sheet.

Example:

0   On sunny afternoons, Maria likes to .... around the lake near her house.

A   visit   **B**   arrive   **C**   walk   *Answer:*

0	A	B	C
	☐	☐	■

---

6   Maria likes to .... a lot of time at the lake.

A   spend   **B**   keep   **C**   stay

7   The water there is warm and beautifully ....

A   light   **B**   clear   **C**   nice

8   In the summer, Maria sometimes .... swimming in the lake.

A   goes   **B**   plays   **C**   wants

9   Some beautiful flowers .... near the lake.

A   stand   **B**   live   **C**   grow

10   When she goes to the lake, Maria usually takes some .... with her.

A   food   **B**   meal   **C**   dish

PART 3

QUESTIONS 11–15

Complete the five conversations.
For questions 11–15, mark A, B or C on your answer sheet.

Example:

0

Where do you come from?

A New York.

B School.

C Home.

Answer: **0** A B C

---

11 Shall we invite Mary to stay next weekend?
    A You decide.
    B It's for you.
    C You make it.

12 When can we meet again?
    A When are you free?
    B It was two days ago.
    C Can you help me?

13 Why don't we eat out in a restaurant tonight?
    A That's a good idea.
    B I hope so.
    C What a pity.

14 We'll have to meet outside the stadium.
    A Can you do it?
    B Have you?
    C At what time?

15 Can I try this shoe in a larger size, please?
    A That'll be very nice.
    B Let me check for you.
    C I can't understand it.

QUESTIONS 16–20

Complete the conversation between Kate and her mother.

What does Kate say to her mother?

For questions 16–20, mark the correct letter A–H on your answer sheet.

Example:

Mother:	Kate, please stop watching TV now and do your homework.

Kate:	0 .... **D**	*Answer:*	0	A B C D E F G H ☐☐☐■☐☐☐☐

Mother:	Sorry. You've got a lot to do tonight. Remember?

Kate:	16 ....

Mother:	That's good. You can help me later, then.

Kate:	17 ....

Mother:	I'm making a cake for Grandma's birthday. You can help with it.

Kate:	18 ....

Mother:	Let's try something different. A lemon one perhaps, if we've got enough lemons.

Kate:	19 ....

Mother:	Good. I think I've got everything else we need.

Kate:	20 ....

Mother:	I'll do that. You finish your homework!

A   Are you sure? Shall I check?

B   I've done some of the homework already, Mum.

C   Great! A chocolate one like last year?

D   Just another half hour, Mum. Please.

E   Oh. What do you want me to do?

F   I made Grandma a birthday card.

G   Can you do that next?

H   There are some in the fridge.

PART 4

QUESTIONS 21–27

Read the article about three piano players.
For questions 21–27, mark A, B or C on your answer sheet.

Piano players – when they were young

Ivan Petrov

Ivan was born on a farm in Russia, but from the age of twelve to eighteen he studied in Poland. His first music teacher couldn't play the piano but taught him and his sister songs from the opera. His mother began to teach him the piano when he was six. At ten, he decided that he wanted to write music too, and he soon started on his first song.

Oleg Gagarin

Oleg was the youngest of five children and when he was four years old his father, who liked playing the piano, taught him some traditional Russian music. When he was six, he started having lessons with a piano teacher who lived in the same city. Oleg soon began to win prizes for his piano playing. At the age of fourteen, he went to a music college in Austria for two years. Later, he returned home to Russia.

Josef Heptmann

Josef's father was German but he taught music in Poland where Josef was born. The family moved to Germany when Josef was two, and a year later he started playing the piano. He gave his first concert when he was six. At ten, he gave fifty-two concerts in two months during a trip to England! Josef always liked music but he was also interested in physics and languages. He is too busy now but one day he would like to write his own music.

Example:

0   Who lived in the countryside when he was young?   **A** Ivan

B Oleg

C Josef

Answer:

---

21   Who had more than one sister or brother?   **A** Ivan

B Oleg

C Josef

22   Who enjoyed other subjects as well as music?   **A** Ivan

B Oleg

C Josef

23   Who studied in another country for two years?   **A** Ivan

B Oleg

C Josef

24   Who was the youngest to begin playing the piano?   **A** Ivan

B Oleg

C Josef

25   Who had music lessons with someone who wasn't
a piano player?   **A** Ivan

B Oleg

C Josef

26   Who did well in music competitions?   **A** Ivan

B Oleg

C Josef

27   Who also wrote music?   **A** Ivan

B Oleg

C Josef

PART 5

QUESTIONS 28–35

Read the article about horse racing.
Choose the best word (A, B or C) for each space.
For questions 28–35, mark A, B or C on your answer sheet.

The history of horse racing

From the first history books **(0)** .... written, it is clear that horse racing has always **(28)** .... an important sport. It started in Central Asia about 4,500 years **(29)** .... and was a favourite sport in both Greek and Roman times.

Modern horse racing began when Arab horses were brought to Europe **(30)** .... the 12th century. At first, races were long and **(31)** .... just two horses, but at the beginning of the 18th century this changed. Races became **(32)** .... shorter and had several horses running against **(33)** .... other.

Today, horse racing **(34)** .... watched by more people than **(35)** .... other sport in the USA, except baseball. It is also very popular in other parts of the world.

Example:

| 0 | **A** already | **B** ever | **C** then | *Answer:* | 0 | A B C |

---

28 **A** be   **B** being   **C** been

29 **A** before   **B** yet   **C** ago

30 **A** in   **B** on   **C** for

31 **A** opposite   **B** through   **C** between

32 **A** many   **B** much   **C** most

33 **A** one   **B** each   **C** every

34 **A** is   **B** are   **C** was

35 **A** some   **B** any   **C** all

PART 6

QUESTIONS 36–40

Read the descriptions of some words about reading and writing.
What is the word for each one?
The first letter is already there. There is one space for each other letter in the word.
For questions 36–40, write the words on your answer sheet.

Example:

0   You may write your appointments in this.   d _ _ _ _

Answer: | **0** | d i a r y |

---

36   This place has many books for you to read, but
      you cannot keep them.   l _ _ _ _ _ _

37   You read this to find out what is happening
      in the world.   n _ _ _ _ _ _ _ _

38   You may need to write this if you answer the
      phone for another person.   m _ _ _ _ _ _

39   The teacher writes on this and everyone in the
      class can see it.   b _ _ _ _

40   If you go on holiday, you may write this and
      send it to a friend.   p _ _ _ _ _ _ _

PART 7

QUESTIONS 41–50

Complete the note.

Write ONE word for each space.

For questions 41–50, write the words on your answer sheet.

Example: | **0** | *a* |

Indre,

I have **(0)** .... problem and I need your help. Can you come shopping **(41)** .... me tomorrow? My grandmother is going to **(42)** .... 80 next month and she is having a party **(43)** .... Saturday.

The problem is I don't have anything to wear. I **(44)** .... grown so much that all my trousers **(45)** .... too short for me now! I want **(46)** .... buy some new ones and maybe a pair **(47)** .... boots. I haven't got a **(48)** .... of money to spend but I think it will be enough.

(49) .... you like to meet me in the morning **(50)** .... the afternoon? Let me know.

Sarika

PART 8

QUESTIONS 51–55

Read the advertisement and the email.
Fill in the information in Sara's notes.
For questions 51–55, write the information on your answer sheet.

Tartan Tours
See Edinburgh with us

Tours of:	Cathedral (10 am)
	Castle (2 pm)
Tickets:	£5.50 (if you book)
	£6.50 (on day)

From: Janet
To: Sara

Sara,

It's too expensive to go by plane to Edinburgh on Friday, so I've got us train tickets. I've booked the Regent Hotel for two nights because the Ashley Hotel was full. Let's do a morning tour on Saturday – can you book the tickets for this? And we'll do the afternoon tour on Sunday.

Sara's notes

Friday	Go to:	Edinburgh
	Travel by:	**51** train
	Name of hotel:	**52**
Saturday	Tour of the:	**53**
	One ticket costs:	**54** £
Sunday	Tour of the:	**55**

PART 9

QUESTION 56

You have just watched a sports competition. Write a note about it to your English friend.

Say:

- **which sport** you watched
- **who** you watched the competition with
- **why** you liked the competition.

Write 25–35 words.
Write the note on your answer sheet.

PAPER 2 LISTENING (approximately 30 minutes including 8 minutes transfer time)

PART 1

QUESTIONS 1–5

You will hear five short conversations.
You will hear each conversation twice.
There is one question for each conversation.
For questions 1–5, put a tick (✔) under the right answer.

Example:

0   How many people were at the meeting?

3	13	30
A ☐	B ☐	C ✔

---

1   Where will the man and woman meet?

A ☐   B ✔   C ☐

2   What's the date of Emma's birthday party?

21st June	20th July	21st July
A ☐	B ☐	C ☐

3 Where is Norah's watch?

A ☑

B ☐

C ☐

4 How much is a ticket for tonight's match?

£3.50

A ☐

£6

B ☐

£10

C ☐

5 Which is the boy's brother?

A ☐

B ☐

C ☐

PART 2

QUESTIONS 6–10

Listen to Amy telling her father about her shopping trip.
What did she and her friends buy?
For questions 6–10, write a letter A–H next to each person.
You will hear the conversation twice.

Example:

0   Amy | H |

People		**Things they bought**
6 Alison	☐	**A** CD
		B magazine
7 Helen	☐	**C** mobile phone
8 Lucy	☐	**D** picture
		E shoes
9 Kerry	☐	**F** suitcase
10 Jo	☐	**G** sweater
		H video

PART 3

QUESTIONS 11–15

Listen to Jamie talking to his mother about a flat.
For questions 11–15, tick (✔) A, B or C.
You will hear the conversation twice.

Example:

0	At the moment, Jamie is living	**A**	at home.	☐
		B	in the university.	✔
		C	in a flat.	☐

11	Jamie will go to university from the new flat	**A**	by bicycle.	☐
		B	by bus.	☐
		C	on foot.	☐
12	The new flat is	**A**	over a shop.	☐
		B	on a noisy road.	☐
		C	next to a café.	☐
13	How much will Jamie pay a week for the flat?	**A**	£200	☐
		B	£40	☐
		C	£14	☐

14   What **doesn't** the flat have?

    A   a cooker   ☐

    B   a fridge   ☐

    C   a washing machine   ☒

15   Jamie agrees to move into the new flat on

    A   Saturday.   ☐

    B   Sunday.   ☒

    C   Monday.   ☐

PART 4

QUESTIONS 16–20

You will hear a woman asking about tickets for the theatre.
Listen and complete questions 16–20.
You will hear the conversation twice.

Theatre tickets

Name of theatre: Queen's

There are tickets for show on:

| 16 | .... evening |

Price for one ticket:

| 17 | £ |

Get tickets from ticket office in:

| 18 | .... Road |

Show starts at:

| 19 | .... p.m. |

Bus number:

| 20 | |

PART 5

QUESTIONS 21–25

You will hear some information about a competition to win a holiday.
Listen and complete questions 21–25.
You will hear the information twice.

Holiday competition

Win a holiday in: *Scotland*

Number of nights: **21** ....

Name of hotel: **22** .... Hotel

At hotel, you can play: **23** ....

Call *The Travel Programme*

Phone before midnight on: **24** ....

Phone number: **25** ....

You now have 8 minutes to write your answers on the answer sheet.

PAPER 3   SPEAKING (8–10 minutes)

The Speaking test lasts 8 to 10 minutes. You will take the test with another candidate. There are two examiners, but only one of them will talk to you. The examiner will ask you questions and ask you to talk to the other candidate.

Part 1 (5–6 minutes)

The examiner will ask you and your partner some questions. These questions will be about your daily life, past experience and future plans. For example, you may have to speak about your school, job, hobbies or home town.

Part 2 (3–4 minutes)

You and your partner will speak to each other. You will ask and answer questions. The examiner will give you a card with some information on it. The examiner will give your partner a card with some words on it. Your partner will use the words on the card to ask you questions about the information you have. Then you will change roles.

Test 3

PAPER 1   READING AND WRITING   (1 hour 10 minutes)

PART 1

QUESTIONS 1–5

Which notice (A–H) says this (1–5)?
For questions 1–5, mark the correct letter A–H on your answer sheet.

Example:

0   This is open all day.

Answer:

0	A	B	C	D	E	F	G	H
	☐	☐	☐	■	☐	☐	☐	☐

---

1   They need someone to work here.

A   Children's book department now on ground floor

2   A special visitor is coming to the shop.

B   **Grey's Books**
Famous children's writer, Michael Whistler, here on Monday 25th

3   Go here if you need help.

C   SALE
All travel books – half price

4   This has moved to a different place.

D   **Coffee shop first floor**
Hot drinks & snacks
9.30–6.30

5   There is a new book on sale.

E   Just arrived! *The Teenage Diaries* by Judy Watson

F   Can't find the right book?
Ask at the information desk

G   WANTED – Sales assistant to help in children's book department

H   *New for customers*
Visit our new website to order your books

PART 2

QUESTIONS 6–10

**Read the sentences about a club for teenagers.
Choose the best word (A, B or C) for each space.
For questions 6–10, mark A, B or C on your
answer sheet.**

Example:

0   Harry Brennan has just joined a club .... Teens Plus.

   A   called   **B**   said   **C**   told   *Answer:*   **0**   A B C

---

6   Teens Plus is a club for young adults who want to ....A............ new friends.

   A   do   **B**   begin   **(C)**   make

7   Harry joined the club when he ....A......... to the town.

   A   moved   **B**   changed   **C**   became

8   There is a ....B........... number of activities to choose from.

   A   tall   **B**   large   **C**   full

9   Last week, everyone went to a restaurant and had a nice ....A........... together.

   (A)   meal   **B**   food   **C**   plate

10   Harry has ....B.......... lots of interesting people at the club.

   A   learnt   **B**   met   **C**   got

PART 3

QUESTIONS 11–15

Complete the five conversations.
For questions 11–15, mark A, B or C on your answer sheet.

Example:

0

Where do you come from?

A New York.

B School.

C Home.

Answer: 0 [A B C]

---

11 I loved the book!

(A) Did you?
B Was it?
C Why not?

12 Would you like some water?

A Yes, of course I do.
(B) Yes, with ice, please.
C Yes, I like it very much.

13 I watched a good film last night.

A What time does it begin?
B Has it finished yet?
(C) What was it called?

14 Do you think Peter will like this sweater?

A He isn't like that.
B You are right.
(C) I'm sure he will.

15 Here, I've found your glasses.

(A) Well done.
B That's all.
C Never mind.

QUESTIONS 16–20

Complete the conversation between two friends.
What does Melissa say to Saskia?
For questions 16–20, mark the correct letter A–H on your answer sheet.

Example:

Saskia: Hello, Melissa, what are you doing this weekend?

Melissa: 0 ....**D**..........   *Answer:* | 0 | A B C **D** E F G H |

Saskia: Oh yes, I've been there.

Melissa: 16 ......**H**......

Saskia: I went to a concert, but I've heard there's a good play on this week.

Melissa: 17 ......**C**......

Saskia: Do you think they've still got tickets for it?

Melissa: 18 ......**A**......

Saskia: Great! I'll book today and call you this evening.

Melissa: 19 ......**F**......

Saskia: Let me check I've got your mobile number.

Melissa: 20 ......**E**......

Saskia: It's OK, I've got it.

A Well, they had lots left yesterday.

B Was it a famous singer?

C That's what I'm going to see on Saturday. Would you like to come?

D I'm going to the new theatre in Bridge Street.

E Shall I give it to you again?

F OK. I'll be home after eight o'clock.

G No, I don't really think so.

H What did you go and see?

PART 4

QUESTIONS 21–27

Read the article about Nick Barlow, who makes travel programmes for television.
Are sentences 21–27 'Right' (A) or 'Wrong' (B)?
If there is not enough information to answer 'Right' (A) or 'Wrong' (B), choose
'Doesn't say' (C).
For questions 21–27, mark A, B or C on your answer sheet.

World traveller

Nick Barlow loves his work. He's a British actor and he travels around the world making TV programmes. 'People welcome me everywhere I go and when I get home I remember all the wonderful things that happened in each country.' Nick has travelled to many places but there are a few trips that he would still like to make. 'I'd love to visit South America and go back to Australia one day,' he says.

On each trip, Nick travels with a team of people. They bring the cameras and other filming equipment needed to make the programme. Nick doesn't take a lot of things for himself, just a few shirts and trousers, but he always makes sure he has some books in his suitcase.

Nick's wife, Helen, doesn't mind him travelling for his work. She has a lot of friends and keeps busy. When he gets back, she likes to listen to all his travel stories. But sometimes there are problems. When he was in the Malaysian rain forest, Nick heard that his wife was ill in hospital. 'I felt terrible because I couldn't help, but she didn't want me to come home. I was so happy when I heard she was better.'

Example:

0   Nick Barlow enjoys his job.

   A   Right   **B**   Wrong   **C**   Doesn't say   *Answer:* | 0 | A B C ■□□ |

---

21   Nick says that people in the places he visits are very friendly.

   (A) Right   **B**   Wrong   **C**   Doesn't say

22   Nick buys something to take home from every country he visits.

   A   Right   **B**   Wrong   **(C)** Doesn't say

23   On some trips, Nick travels alone.

   A   Right   **(B)** Wrong   **C**   Doesn't say

24   There are often problems with the television cameras.

   A   Right   **B**   Wrong   **(C)** Doesn't say

25   Every time Nick goes away, he packs something to read.

   (A) Right   **B**   Wrong   **C**   Doesn't say

26   Helen is unhappy when he's away from home.

   A   Right   **(B)** Wrong   **C**   Doesn't say

27   When Helen was sick, Nick returned home.

   A   Right   **(B)** Wrong   **C**   Doesn't say

PART 5

QUESTIONS 28–35

Read the article about big cats.

Choose the best word (A, B or C) for each space.

For questions 28–35, mark A, B or C on your answer sheet.

Big cats

There are **(0)** .... different kinds of cats. They are different in size and they do not look or act the same.

Tigers are the biggest cats. **(28)** ......A........ head to tail they can be 3.7m long. Most cats don't like water, **(29)** ......C........ tigers will often lie in a pool of water when **(30)** ....it........ is hot!

Lions are the **(31)** ....A........ cats that stay together in large family groups. Several lions may work together to get food for the group. They usually **(32)** ....B........ in flat, open countryside where they can see a long way and easily follow **(33)** ....C........ animals.

(34) ....A........ cats need good eyes, because they catch smaller animals for their food. They also need to be fast, and **(35)** ....B........ strong.

Example:

0	**A** many	**B** much	**C** more			

Answer: 0 | A ■ | B ☐ | C ☐ |

---

28 **A** From   **B** At   **C** By

29 **A** so   **B** if   **C** but

30 **A** he   **B** they   **C** it

31 **A** only   **B** just   **C** once

32 **A** living   **B** live   **C** lives

33 **A** another   **B** any   **C** other

34 **A** All   **B** Every   **C** Each

35 **A** too   **B** very   **C** even

PART 6

QUESTIONS 36–40

Read the descriptions of some buildings in a town.
What is the word for each one?
The first letter is already there. There is one space for each other letter in the word.
For questions 36–40, write the words on your answer sheet.

Example:

0   This is where a company makes the things that it sells.   f _ _ _ _ _ _

Answer: | **0** | f a c t o r y |

---

36   People can study different things here.   c OLLEGE

37   You can look at very old things here.   m u S E U M

38   You may need to buy a ticket before you go on the   s T A T I O N
platform here.

39   In this place, a waiter will bring you your meal.   r E S T A U R A N T

40   You can go here to watch a big match.   s T A D I U M

PART 7

QUESTIONS 41–50

Complete the letter.
Write ONE word for each space.
For questions 41–50, write the words on your answer sheet.

Example: | **0** | y o u |

Dear Deshini,

It's great that **(0)** .... are my new penfriend. My name is Tom and I
(41) ...AM.... fifteen years old. I **(42)** ...was... born in Canada but I live in
England now. Please write and tell me all **(43)** ...About.. your life in India.
I **(44)** ...would..love to go there one day.

Do you live in a small village **(45)** ...or.. in a big town? **(46)** ...What.. is your
school like? **(47)** ...Have... you got any pictures of your school you could send
me? I'm sending you **(48)** ......a...... few photos of my family. I'll send more the
(49) ...Next.. time I write.

I hope you'll write **(50)** ......to.... me soon.

Tom

PART 8

QUESTIONS 51–55

Read the advertisement and the email.

Fill in the information in Marina's notes.

For questions 51–55, write the information on your answer sheet.

RIVERSIDE SPORTS CLUB
CLASSES
Swimming
Thursday or Sunday
2 p.m. and 7 p.m.
Tennis
Thursday or Saturday
2 p.m. and 8 p.m.
Price of courses:
Daytime   £20
Evenings   £30

From:	Vika
To:	Marina

Could you book a sports course for the three of us – us two and Ali? Let's have tennis lessons – we can do swimming in the summer. The weekend isn't good for me – it has to be Thursday. Also, Ali's music lesson is at 2 p.m. so we have to do the later class. It costs more, but never mind.

Marina's notes
Sports course

Where:	Riverside Sports Club
Which sport:	**51** Tennis
Day:	**52** THURSDAY
Time:	**53** .... p.m.
Number of people:	**54** 3
Cost each:	**55** £ 30

PART 9

QUESTION 56

You went shopping for clothes yesterday. Write a postcard to a friend.

Say:

- **what clothes** you bought
- **why** you bought them
- **how much** they cost.

Write 25–35 words.
Write the postcard on your answer sheet.

PAPER 2 LISTENING (approximately 30 minutes including 8 minutes transfer time)

PART 1

QUESTIONS 1–5

You will hear five short conversations.
You will hear each conversation twice.
There is one question for each conversation.
For questions 1–5, put a tick (✔) under the right answer.

Example:

0 How many people were at the meeting?

3	**13**	**30**
A ☐	B ☐	C ☑

---

1 Which boy is Peter?

A ☐   B ☐   C ☐

2 Which day will they go to the cinema?

Tuesday	**Wednesday**	**Thursday**
A ☐	B ☐	C ☐

3 What are they going to do on Saturday?

A ☑ B ☐ C ☑

4 Where does Paul live?

A ☐ B ☐ C ☐

5 Where are they going to put the computer?

A ☑ B ☐ C ☐

PART 2

QUESTIONS 6–10

Listen to Janet talking to her friend about a party.
What did each person wear?
For questions 6–10, write a letter A–H next to each person.
You will hear the conversation twice.

Example:

0	Janet	E

People

Clothes

6 Emma

7 Mike

8 Michelle

9 Rachel

10 Jason

A blouse

B dress

C jacket

D jeans

E skirt

F suit

G sweater

H T-shirt

PART 3

QUESTIONS 11–15

Listen to Zak talking to Maria about his sports bag.
For questions 11–15, tick (✔) A, B or C.
You will hear the conversation twice.

Example:

0	What colour is Zak's bag?	A	blue	✔
		B	white	☐
		C	black	☐

11	The bag is	A	small.	☐
		B	old.	☐
		C	dirty.	☐

12	Where is the bag?	A	in the classroom	☐
		B	on the sports field	☐
		C	at the hospital	☐

13	What is inside the bag?	A	money	☐
		B	a watch	☐
		C	clothes	☐

14   Maria should take the bag to Zak

       A   this afternoon. ☐

       B   this evening. ☐

       C   tomorrow morning. ☐

15   Zak hurt himself when he was

       A   playing football. ☐

       B   running. ☐

       C   changing his clothes. ☐

PART 4

QUESTIONS 16–20

You will hear a man asking for some information about a swimming pool.
Listen and complete questions 16–20.
You will hear the conversation twice.

Swimming pool

Closing day:	Monday
The 'early morning swim' starts at:	**16** .... a.m.
9.30–12.30, pool is used by:	**17**
Each lesson costs:	**18** £
Date of next course:	**19**
Teacher's name:	**20** Roy ....

PART 5

QUESTIONS 21–25

You will hear some information about free cinema tickets.
Listen and complete questions 21–25.
You will hear the information twice.

Free cinema tickets

Usual price:	£5
Name of film:	**21** The Elephant ....
Send postcard to:	Radio South-West
Address:	**22** 27 .... Road, Bristol
Before:	**23** .... July
Number of tickets per family:	**24**
Everybody will get a:	**25**

You now have 8 minutes to write your answers on the answer sheet.

PAPER 3   SPEAKING (8–10 minutes)

The Speaking test lasts 8 to 10 minutes. You will take the test with another candidate. There are two examiners, but only one of them will talk to you. The examiner will ask you questions and ask you to talk to the other candidate.

Part 1 (5–6 minutes)

The examiner will ask you and your partner some questions. These questions will be about your daily life, past experience and future plans. For example, you may have to speak about your school, job, hobbies or home town.

Part 2 (3–4 minutes)

You and your partner will speak to each other. You will ask and answer questions. The examiner will give you a card with some information on it. The examiner will give your partner a card with some words on it. Your partner will use the words on the card to ask you questions about the information you have. Then you will change roles.

Test 4

PAPER 1   READING AND WRITING   (1 hour 10 minutes)

PART 1

QUESTIONS 1–5

Which notice (A–H) says this (1–5)?
For questions 1–5, mark the correct letter A–H on your answer sheet.

Example:

0   You must not eat here.

Answer:

0	A	B	C	D	E	F	G	H
	☐	☐	☐	☐	☐	☐	☐	■

---

1   You cannot come here tomorrow.

A   JULES FOURNIER PLAYS CLASSICAL GUITAR Students half price

2   If you want to play music well, you can study here.

B   The ABC cinema closes for two weeks today for repairs

3   You will have to pay more if you come to this place tomorrow.

C   SUMMERTOWN SCHOOL NO TICKETS LEFT FOR NEXT WEEK'S CONCERT

D   NEW THEATRE RESTAURANT Meals half price today only

4   You can get cheaper tickets if you are at college.

E   Music Shop Closed for lunch

F   Piano and guitar courses at City College Beginners welcome

5   You can buy music more cheaply here for a short time.

G   MUSIC STORE Low prices on latest CDs Next two weeks only

H   Please do not take any food or drink into theatre

PART 2

QUESTIONS 6–10

Read the sentences about horse-riding lessons.
Choose the best word (A, B or C) for each space.
For questions 6–10, mark A, B or C on your answer sheet.

Example:

0   Sam .... horse-riding lessons every Saturday morning.

    A   goes   **B**   has   **C**   makes   *Answer:* **0**   A B C ▢ ■ ▢

---

6   Sam .... to ride when he was seven years old.

    A   knew   **B**   practised   **C**   learnt

7   He has to wear a special riding hat to keep himself ....

    A   safe   **B**   careful   **C**   sure

8   Sam got first .... at a riding competition last week.

    A   time   **B**   race   **C**   prize

9   He .... that one day he will have his own horse.

    A   wants   **B**   hopes   **C**   likes

10   Sam is doing a Saturday job to try to .... enough money to buy his own horse.

    A   earn   **B**   pay   **C**   spend

PART 3

QUESTIONS 11–15

Complete the five conversations.
For questions 11–15, mark A, B or C on your answer sheet.

Example:

0

Where do you come from?

A New York.

B School.

C Home.

Answer: 0 A B C

---

11 It's too cold today.

A It's all day.

B It will be warmer tomorrow.

C No, I don't like it.

12 Have you seen John?

A He's just gone out.

B I don't mind where.

C He's happy to do that.

13 Please tell Liz I'll call her again this evening.

A I haven't called her.

B I'll leave a note.

C I don't know.

14 Can you all give me your homework now?

A Not since Friday.

B It's easier than mine.

C I've only done one page.

15 You're looking really well.

A Never mind.

B Do you think so?

C It doesn't matter.

QUESTIONS 16–20

Complete the conversation in a shop.
What does Tanya say to the shop assistant?
For questions 16–20, mark the correct letter A–H on your answer sheet.

Example:

Assistant:	Good afternoon. Can I help you?
Tanya:	0 .... **H** ....

Answer:

0	A	B	C	D	E	F	G	H
	☐	☐	☐	☐	☐	☐	☐	■

Assistant:	We've only got two left. Would you like to try them on?
Tanya:	16 .... A ....
Assistant:	I agree, but it's too small for you. What about this one?
Tanya:	17 .... E ....
Assistant:	That's a pity. That's all the ski hats we've got.
Tanya:	18 .... B ....
Assistant:	There's one near the chemist's.
Tanya:	19 .... G ....
Assistant:	That's right. If they haven't got any, try the sports shop on Harrey Street.
Tanya:	20 .... C ....
Assistant:	You're welcome. Goodbye.

A Thanks. This one's a nice colour.

B Is there another shop that sells them?

C I'll do that. Thanks a lot.

D I'm not sure how to get there.

E I don't think it will look right with my red ski jacket.

F Have you got a bigger one?

G Is it on the ground floor of the shopping centre, by the entrance?

H Yes, I'm looking for a ski hat.

PART 4

QUESTIONS 21–27

Read the article about Indian films.
Are sentences 21–27 'Right' (A) or 'Wrong' (B)?
If there is not enough information to answer 'Right' (A) or 'Wrong' (B), choose 'Doesn't say' (C).
For questions 21–27, mark A, B or C on your answer sheet.

Bollywood

'Bollywood', which is the name of the film industry in Mumbai, India, makes almost 1,000 films a year. Since making its first film in 1913, Bollywood has made over 29,000 films. This is a much higher number than the USA and means it is the biggest film industry in the world. Most Indians like watching films better than any other free-time activity and ten million of them go to the cinema every day. Bollywood films tell romantic love stories, and singing and dancing are an important part of every film. Indian films are also enjoyed outside India. Last year, Bollywood made over $500 million by selling its films to other countries.

Indian actors make more films each year than American actors in Hollywood, but they are not paid as much. This is why most Bollywood films only cost about $2 million to make. A Hollywood film is never made for under $5 million.

Most Bollywood actors are young. They work hard but only for a few years. Amitabh Bachchan, who some people say is India's greatest actor, is different. He has been the star of more than 140 films during an acting career of almost 40 years.

Example:

0   The Indian film industry is called Bollywood.

    A   Right   **B**   Wrong   **C**   Doesn't say   *Answer:*   0   A B C

---

21   Since 1913, Bollywood has made just under 29,000 films.

    A   Right   **B**   Wrong   **C**   Doesn't say

22   A lot more films are made in India than in the USA.

    A   Right   **B**   Wrong   **C**   Doesn't say

23   Going to the cinema is most Indians' favourite hobby.

    A   Right   **B**   Wrong   **C**   Doesn't say

24   Bollywood spends a lot of money on advertisements to sell its films.

    A   Right   **B**   Wrong   **C**   Doesn't say

25   Films are cheaper to make in Bollywood than in Hollywood.

    A   Right   **B**   Wrong   **C**   Doesn't say

26   Most Bollywood actors work in films until they are quite old.

    A   Right   **B**   Wrong   **C**   Doesn't say

27   Many young Indian actors would like to work with the Bollywood star Amitabh Bachchan.

    A   Right   **B**   Wrong   **C**   Doesn't say

PART 5

QUESTIONS 28–35

Read the article about buildings.
Choose the best word (A, B or C) for each space.
For questions 28–35, mark A, B or C on your answer sheet.

Buildings

People **(0)** ......HAVE.... always made buildings. We need houses to keep us warm and dry and we build stadiums **(28)** ....SO....... we can watch football matches and pop concerts. We use **(29)** ...OTHER.. buildings, like museums, to keep beautiful things in.

(30) ..MANY... people work together on a building. The architect decides how the building is going to look and draws pictures that show people his or her ideas. Engineers make sure the building will **(31)** .....be....... strong and safe. Then, the workers carefully build **(32)** .....THEM. .

The Sydney Opera House is a famous modern building with a lovely roof. But the building is beautiful from **(33)** ..EVERY.. side, not only from the top. There is also a famous roof on the Olympic Stadium **(34)** .....in..... Munich. This interesting building looks like a tent that is **(35)** ..made. of glass.

Example:

0   **A**   having   **B**   has   **C**   have   *Answer:* | 0 | A B C ☐☐■ |

---

28   **A**   or   **B**   but   **C**   so

29   **A**   other   **B**   each   **C**   another

30   **A**   Much   **B**   More   **C**   Many

31   **A**   be   **B**   was   **C**   been

32   **A**   them   **B**   it   **C**   her

33   **A**   some   **B**   every   **C**   both

34   **A**   in   **B**   on   **C**   from

35   **A**   made   **B**   make   **C**   making

PART 6

QUESTIONS 36–40

Read the descriptions of some words for jobs. What is the word for each one?
The first letter is already there. There is one space for each other letter in the word.
For questions 36–40, write the words on your answer sheet.

Example:

0   You go to see this person if you are ill.   d __ __ __ __ __

	Answer:	**0**	d o c t o r

---

36   This person lives in the countryside where he grows food and keeps animals.

f A R M E R

37   If you have a problem with your car, this person can repair it.

m E C H A N I C

38   This person writes for a newspaper.

j O U R N A L I S T

39   You speak to this person when you ask for a meal in a restaurant.

w A I T E R

40   This person uses a camera in his work.

p H O T O G R A P H E R

fotografo

PART 7

QUESTIONS 41–50

Complete the letter.
Write ONE word for each space.
For questions 41–50, write the words on your answer sheet.

Example: | **0** | f o r |

Dear Keira,

Thank you **(0)** ...*for*... your letter. I had my first day **(41)** ...*in*... my new school today. A girl **(42)** *called* Nicole looked after me and showed me **(43)** *where* my classrooms were. She is very nice and I **(44)** ...*am*... going to visit her this weekend.

My favourite lesson today was Maths and I was happy because I knew more **(45)** ...*than* the other girls. I also played hockey for **(46)** ...*the*... first time. I really enjoyed it.

Most of the teachers seem friendly but I'm afraid **(47)** ...*of*... the head teacher. No one likes **(48)** ...*him*... because he shouts **(49)** ...*a*... lot.

I must go now because I have **(50)** ...*to*... do my homework.

Hester

PART 8

QUESTIONS 51–55

Read the advertisement and the email.
Fill in the information in Nina's notes.
For questions 51–55, write the information on your answer sheet.

EUROPA RESTAURANT

Italian food
Monday – Tuesday

Greek food
Wednesday – Sunday

35 seats

Open 7 p.m. – midnight

Dinner – £25 per person (£20 for groups of ten or more)

From: Susie
To: Nina

It's Bella's birthday next week. What about Europa Restaurant for her birthday party? Can you book a table for eighteen of us?

She prefers Italian food to Greek food and she's not free on Monday so let's go there next Tuesday. 7 p.m. is early, so say half past when you phone.

Thanks.

Nina's notes
Book table for Bella's party

Restaurant:	Europa
Day:	**51** TUESDAY
Type of food wanted:	**52** ITALIAN FOOD
Time:	**53** 7:30 p.m.
Number of people:	**54** 18
Price per person:	**55** £ 20

PART 9

QUESTION 56

Read this note from your friend, Sarah.

> Yes, I would like to play tennis this evening.
>
> What time shall we meet at your house? How are we going to get to the sports centre? What do I need to wear?

Write a note to Sarah and answer her questions.
Write 25–35 words.
Write the note on your answer sheet.

PAPER 2 LISTENING (approximately 30 minutes including 8 minutes transfer time)

PART 1

QUESTIONS 1–5

You will hear five short conversations.

You will hear each conversation twice.

There is one question for each conversation.

For questions 1–5, put a tick (✔) under the right answer.

Example:

0 How many people were at the meeting?

3	**13**	**30**
A ☐	B ☐	C ✔

---

1 What are the boys going to do?

A ☑

B ☐   C ☐

2 Which tent does the girl choose?

A ☑

B ☐   C ☐

3 Which one is Ruth's bike?

A ☐

B ☐

C ☑

4 What does Sarah's dad do?

A ☐

B ☐

C ☐

5 Which picture is the woman asking about?

A ☐

B ☑

C ☐

PART 2

QUESTIONS 6–10

Listen to Kerri talking to a friend about her new room.
Where do they decide to put her things?
For questions 6–10, write a letter A–H next to each thing.
You will hear the conversation twice.

Example:

0	computer	**D**

Things

6 books

7 plant

8 lamp

9 pillow

10 toy bear

Places

A bed

B big cupboard

C small cupboard

D desk

E floor

F shelf

G sofa

H table

PART 3

QUESTIONS 11–15

Listen to Jim talking to Sarah about things to take on holiday.
For questions 11–15, tick (✔) A, B or C.
You will hear the conversation twice.

Example:

0 Last month, Jim went to

A	Italy.	☐
B	England.	☐
C	Austria.	✔

---

11 Where did Jim buy his walking shoes?

A	at the market	☐
B	in a supermarket	☐
C	in a shoe shop	☐

12 The shoes cost Jim

A	£20.	☐
B	£48.	☐
C	£68.	☐

13 Jim says Sarah should take

A	a jacket.	☐
B	a sweater.	☐
C	a sun hat.	☐

14 How many T-shirts should Sarah take?

    A   one ☐

    B   five ☑

    C   seven ☐

15 Sarah should take her phone because she may want to

    A   phone the hotel. ☐

    B   phone home. ☐

    C   phone for help. ☑

PART 4

QUESTIONS 16–20

You will hear Sally asking a friend about some homework.
Listen and complete questions 16–20.
You will hear the conversation twice.

Homework

Subject:	Biology
Name of book:	**16**
Written by:	**17** Martin
Read:	**18** pages
Learn about:	**19**
Finish by:	**20**

PART 5

QUESTIONS 21–25

You will hear some information on the radio about a summer music school.
Listen and complete questions 21–25.
You will hear the information twice.

Summer music school

Place: Arts Centre

Starting date: **21** .... July

Learn to play: **22** piano, guitar, ...

Classes start at: **23** .... a.m.

Cost of classes: **24** £ .... a day

Phone number: **25**

You now have 8 minutes to write your answers on the answer sheet.

PAPER 3   SPEAKING (8–10 minutes)

The Speaking test lasts 8 to 10 minutes. You will take the test with another candidate. There are two examiners, but only one of them will talk to you. The examiner will ask you questions and ask you to talk to the other candidate.

Part 1 (5–6 minutes)

The examiner will ask you and your partner some questions. These questions will be about your daily life, past experience and future plans. For example, you may have to speak about your school, job, hobbies or home town.

Part 2 (3–4 minutes)

You and your partner will speak to each other. You will ask and answer questions. The examiner will give you a card with some information on it. The examiner will give your partner a card with some words on it. Your partner will use the words on the card to ask you questions about the information you have. Then you will change roles.

Visual materials for Paper 3

1A

Animal World Zoo

Open every day of the year
9.00 am – 6.00 pm

elephants, lions, bears and much more

Adults £12   Children £6

2 kilometres from town centre

2B

Car museum

◆ **very old cars?**

◆ **time / close?**

◆ **open / weekends?**

◆ **address?**

◆ **more information? ☎?**

3A

SCHOOL PICNIC

All students welcome
Next Sunday
in Spring Park

Free sandwiches and cakes
Bring some drinks

Bus leaves school 12.30 pm

4B

School play

◆ **name / play?**

◆ **where?**

◆ **writer?**

◆ **ticket? £?**

◆ **date?**

1B

Zoo

♦ **name / zoo?**

♦ **where?**

♦ **child's ticket? £?**

♦ **what animals?**

♦ **open tomorrow?**

2A

CAR MUSEUM
36 Spring Road

Open every day of the year

10 am – 6 pm

Cars from 1890 until today

Entrance free

For information: ☎ 723619

3B

<u>School picnic</u>

◆ **where / picnic?**

◆ **when?**

◆ **for everybody?**

◆ **go by bus?**

◆ **bring food?**

4A

Come and see our play!
in
the Queen Mary School
on 10th July

The Storm
Written by students in Class 8
Get your tickets now!
£2.50

1C

HORSE FOR SALE

£500 to a good home

Six years old
Brown with white face

Small and friendly — good for children
Call Garden Farm on 997551

2D

Castle

- ◆ **name / castle?**

- ◆ **age?**

- ◆ **restaurant?**

- ◆ **family ticket? £?**

- ◆ **car park?**

3C

Ride on the Mountain Train

Go to the top of Silver Mountain
See the beautiful lakes

A 3-hour journey to remember!

Tickets £11
Every day – 2 pm

4D

College shop

♦ **open every day?**

♦ **what / buy?**

♦ **low prices?**

♦ **where?**

♦ **closing time?**

1D

Horse for sale

♦ **big horse?**

♦ **colour?**

♦ **price?**

♦ **age?**

♦ **more information? ☎?**

2C

Visit Greystone Castle

Over 500 years old

Tickets: £4
Family Ticket: £12

Castle shop with postcards, snacks and drinks

Free parking

3D

Mountain train ride

- where / go?

- on Saturdays?

- what / see?

- long journey?

- price? £?

4C

New COLLEGE SHOP
opposite Library

This week only – everything half price
Monday – Saturday
8 am – 8 pm

For paper, pens, bags . . . and more!

Manager: Tom Green

Paper 3 frames

Test 1

Note: The visual materials for Paper 3 appear on pages 94–101.

Part 1 (5–6 minutes)

Greetings and introductions

At the beginning of Part 1, the interlocutor greets the candidates, asks for their names and asks them to spell something.

Giving information about place of origin, occupation, studies

The interlocutor asks the candidates about where they come from / live, and for information about their school/studies/work.

Giving general information about self

The interlocutor asks the candidates questions about their daily life, past experience or future plans. They may be asked, for example, about their likes and dislikes or about recent past experiences, or to describe and compare places.

Extended response

In the final section of Part 1, candidates are expected to give an extended response to a 'Tell me something about . . .' prompt. The topics are still of a personal and concrete nature. Candidates should produce at least three utterances in their extended response.

Part 2 (3–4 minutes)

The interlocutor introduces the activity as follows:

Interlocutor: (*Pablo*), here is some information about a zoo.

(*Interlocutor shows answer card 1A on page 94 to Pablo.*)

(*Laura*), you don't know anything about the zoo, so ask (*Pablo*) some questions about it.

(*Interlocutor shows question card 1B on page 96 to Laura.*)

Use these words to help you. (*Interlocutor indicates prompt words.*)

Do you understand?

Now, (*Laura*), ask (*Pablo*) your questions about the zoo, and (*Pablo*), you answer them.

1A

Animal World Zoo

Open every day of the year

9.00 am – 6.00 pm

elephants, lions, bears and much more

Adults £12   Children £6

2 kilometres from town centre

1B

Zoo

♦ **name / zoo?**

♦ **where?**

♦ **child's ticket? £?**

♦ **what animals?**

♦ **open tomorrow?**

When the candidates have asked and answered questions about the zoo, they exchange roles and talk about a different topic.

The interlocutor introduces the activity as follows:

Interlocutor: (*Laura*), here is some information about a horse for sale.

(*Interlocutor shows answer card 1C on page 98 to Laura.*)

(*Pablo*), you don't know anything about the horse, so ask (*Laura*) some questions about it.

(*Interlocutor shows question card 1D on page 100 to Pablo.*)

Use these words to help you. (*Interlocutor indicates prompt words.*)

Do you understand?

Now, (*Pablo*), ask (*Laura*) your questions about the horse, and (*Laura*), you answer them.

1C

HORSE FOR SALE

£500 to a good home

Six years old
Brown with white face

Small and friendly — good for children

Call Garden Farm on 997551

1D

Horse for sale

♦ **big horse?**

♦ **colour?**

♦ **price?**

♦ **age?**

♦ **more information? ☎?**

Note: Candidates are assessed on both their questions and answers in Part 2 of the test.

Test 2

Note: The visual materials for Paper 3 appear on pages 94–101.

Part 1 (5–6 minutes)

Greetings and introductions

At the beginning of Part 1, the interlocutor greets the candidates, asks for their names and asks them to spell something.

Giving information about place of origin, occupation, studies

The interlocutor asks the candidates about where they come from / live, and for information about their school/studies/work.

Giving general information about self

The interlocutor asks the candidates questions about their daily life, past experience or future plans. They may be asked, for example, about their likes and dislikes or about recent past experiences, or to describe and compare places.

Extended response

In the final section of Part 1, candidates are expected to give an extended response to a 'Tell me something about . . .' prompt. The topics are still of a personal and concrete nature. Candidates should produce at least three utterances in their extended response.

Part 2 (3–4 minutes)

The interlocutor introduces the activity as follows:

Interlocutor: (*Pablo*), here is some information about a car museum.

(*Interlocutor shows answer card 2A on page 96 to Pablo.*)

(*Laura*), you don't know anything about the car museum, so ask (*Pablo*) some questions about it.

(*Interlocutor shows question card 2B on page 94 to Laura.*)

Use these words to help you. (*Interlocutor indicates prompt words.*)

Do you understand?

Now, (*Laura*), ask (*Pablo*) your questions about the car museum, and (*Pablo*), you answer them.

2A

CAR MUSEUM
36 Spring Road

Open every day of the year

10 am – 6 pm

Cars from 1890 until today

Entrance free

For information: ☎ 723619

2B

Car museum

♦ **very old cars?**

♦ **time / close?**

♦ **open / weekends?**

♦ **address?**

♦ **more information? ☎?**

When the candidates have asked and answered questions about the car museum, they exchange roles and talk about a different topic.

The interlocutor introduces the activity as follows:

Interlocutor: (*Laura*), here is some information about a visit to a castle.

(*Interlocutor shows answer card 2C on page 100 to Laura.*)

(*Pablo*), you don't know anything about the visit to the castle, so ask (*Laura*) some questions about it.

(*Interlocutor shows question card 2D on page 98 to Pablo.*)

Use these words to help you. (*Interlocutor indicates prompt words.*)

Do you understand?

Now, (*Pablo*), ask (*Laura*) your questions about the visit to the castle, and (*Laura*), you answer them.

2C

Visit Greystone Castle

Over 500 years old

Tickets: £4
Family Ticket: £12

Castle shop with postcards, snacks and drinks
Free parking

2D

Castle

♦ **name / castle?**

♦ **age?**

♦ **restaurant?**

♦ **family ticket? £?**

♦ **car park?**

Note: Candidates are assessed on both their questions and answers in Part 2 of the test.

Test 3

Note: The visual materials for Paper 3 appear on pages 94–101.

Part 1 (5–6 minutes)

Greetings and introductions

At the beginning of Part 1, the interlocutor greets the candidates, asks for their names and asks them to spell something.

Giving information about place of origin, occupation, studies

The interlocutor asks the candidates about where they come from / live, and for information about their school/studies/work.

Giving general information about self

The interlocutor asks the candidates questions about their daily life, past experience or future plans. They may be asked, for example, about their likes and dislikes or about recent past experiences, or to describe and compare places.

Extended response

In the final section of Part 1, candidates are expected to give an extended response to a 'Tell me something about . . .' prompt. The topics are still of a personal and concrete nature. Candidates should produce at least three utterances in their extended response.

Part 2 (3–4 minutes)

The interlocutor introduces the activity as follows:

Interlocutor: (*Pablo*), here is some information about a school picnic.

(*Interlocutor shows answer card 3A on page 95 to Pablo.*)

(*Laura*), you don't know anything about the school picnic, so ask (*Pablo*) some questions about it.

(*Interlocutor shows question card 3B on page 97 to Laura.*)

Use these words to help you. (*Interlocutor indicates prompt words.*)

Do you understand?

Now, (*Laura*), ask (*Pablo*) your questions about the school picnic, and (*Pablo*), you answer them.

3A

SCHOOL PICNIC

All students welcome
Next Sunday
in Spring Park

Free sandwiches and cakes
Bring some drinks

Bus leaves school 12.30 pm

3B

School picnic

♦ **where / picnic?**

♦ **when?**

♦ **for everybody?**

♦ **go by bus?**

♦ **bring food?**

When the candidates have asked and answered questions about the school picnic, they exchange roles and talk about a different topic.

The interlocutor introduces the activity as follows:

Interlocutor: (*Laura*), here is some information about a mountain train ride.

(*Interlocutor shows answer card 3C on page 99 to Laura.*)

(*Pablo*), you don't know anything about the mountain train ride, so ask (*Laura*) some questions about it.

(*Interlocutor shows question card 3D on page 101 to Pablo.*)

Use these words to help you. (*Interlocutor indicates prompt words.*)

Do you understand?

Now, (*Pablo*), ask (*Laura*) your questions about the mountain train ride, and (*Laura*), you answer them.

3C

Ride on the Mountain Train

Go to the top of Silver Mountain
See the beautiful lakes

A 3-hour journey to remember!
Tickets £11
Every day – 2 pm

3D

Mountain train ride

♦ **where / go?**

♦ **on Saturdays?**

♦ **what / see?**

♦ **long journey?**

♦ **price? £?**

Note: Candidates are assessed on both their questions and answers in Part 2 of the test.

Test 4

Note: The visual materials for Paper 3 appear on pages 94–101.

Part 1 (5–6 minutes)

Greetings and introductions

At the beginning of Part 1, the interlocutor greets the candidates, asks for their names and asks them to spell something.

Giving information about place of origin, occupation, studies

The interlocutor asks the candidates about where they come from / live, and for information about their school/studies/work.

Giving general information about self

The interlocutor asks the candidates questions about their daily life, past experience or future plans. They may be asked, for example, about their likes and dislikes or about recent past experiences, or to describe and compare places.

Extended response

In the final section of Part 1, candidates are expected to give an extended response to a 'Tell me something about . . .' prompt. The topics are still of a personal and concrete nature. Candidates should produce at least three utterances in their extended response.

Part 2 (3–4 minutes)

The interlocutor introduces the activity as follows:

Interlocutor: (*Pablo*), here is some information about a school play.

(*Interlocutor shows answer card 4A on page 97 to Pablo.*)

(*Laura*), you don't know anything about the school play, so ask (*Pablo*) some questions about it.

(*Interlocutor shows question card 4B on page 95 to Laura.*)

Use these words to help you. (*Interlocutor indicates prompt words.*)

Do you understand?

Now, (*Laura*), ask (*Pablo*) your questions about the school play, and (*Pablo*), you answer them.

4A

Come and see our play!
in
the Queen Mary School
on 10th July

The Storm

Written by students in Class 8

Get your tickets now!

£2.50

4B

School play

♦ **name / play?**

♦ **where?**

♦ **writer?**

♦ **ticket? £?**

♦ **date?**

When the candidates have asked and answered questions about the school play, they exchange roles and talk about a different topic.

The interlocutor introduces the activity as follows:

Interlocutor: (*Laura*), here is some information about a college shop.

(*Interlocutor shows answer card 4C on page 101 to Laura.*)

(*Pablo*), you don't know anything about the college shop, so ask (*Laura*) some questions about it.

(*Interlocutor shows question card 4D on page 99 to Pablo.*)

Use these words to help you. (*Interlocutor indicates prompt words.*)

Do you understand?

Now, (*Pablo*), ask (*Laura*) your questions about the college shop, and (*Laura*), you answer them.

4C

New COLLEGE SHOP
opposite Library

This week only – everything half price

**Monday – Saturday
8 am – 8 pm**

For paper, pens, bags . . . and more!

Manager: Tom Green

4D

College shop

♦ **open every day?**

♦ **what / buy?**

♦ **low prices?**

♦ **where?**

♦ **closing time?**

Note: Candidates are assessed on both their questions and answers in Part 2 of the test.

Test 1 Key

Paper 1   Reading and Writing

Part 1

1 E   **2** D   **3** G   **4** B   **5** A

Part 2

6 A   **7** B   **8** C   **9** C   **10** B

Part 3

11 A   **12** A   **13** C   **14** C   **15** B
16 C   **17** F   **18** H   **19** E   **20** B

Part 4

21 A   **22** B   **23** B   **24** C   **25** B   **26** A   **27** C

Part 5

28 C   **29** C   **30** B   **31** C   **32** A   **33** A   **34** B   **35** B

Part 6

For questions 36–40, spelling must be correct.

36 tent   **37** guitar   **38** magazines   **39** boots   **40** video

Part 7

For questions 41–50, ignore capitals / absence of capitals. Spelling must be correct.

41 a   **42** than/because   **43** with   **44** go   **45** up   **46** to
47 me/anyone/us   **48** it   **49** her   **50** if/when

Part 8

For questions 51–55, spelling must be correct.

51 Storm   **52** 11(.00) / eleven (o'clock) (am / in the morning) NOT pm
53 (Sunday) 23(rd) / twenty(-)third June   **54** 3   **55** (£)6(.00) / six (pounds)

Part 9

Question 56

The three pieces of information that must be communicated are:

i   what the writer likes about the mobile phone

ii   what it cost

iii   its colour.

Sample answer A

Mark: 5

> Hi Mike! My new mobile is fantastic!
> The best of it is its camera. It has got five mega pixels.
> It's too exspensive. It cost 400£ I've chosen my fovorit black colour.
> I love it. Now I have to buy some cheese.
> See you soon, XXX
> Alex

All three parts of the message are clearly communicated with only minor spelling errors.

Sample answer B

Mark: 4

> Dear Mike,
> my new mobile phone is Nokia 5500, it cost's $49.00 and it's a black. I
> prefer it is very small and I like. My number is 01112 1122111, please call me
> now.
> Bye, Jan

All three parts of the message are clearly communicated with some awkwardness of
expression.

Sample answer C

Mark: 3

> HI MIKE,
> MY NEW MOBILE PHONE IS VERY BEAUTIFUL BECAUSE IT'S VERY
> SMALL. ITS COLOUR IS BLACK BECAUSE IS MY FAVOURITE COLOUR. OK
> WRITE ME SOON. BYE.

Two parts of the message are clearly communicated (the response does not address
how much the phone cost).

Sample answer D

Mark: 3

> *To: Mike*
> *From: Dan*
> *I would like to bought your mobile phone. I would like it because it's very*
> *small. I want a black colour about it. It cost £50.00.*
> *I hope you will sell it.*
> *See you soon,*
> *Vivien.*

All three parts of the message are included but the context is incorrect.

Sample answer E

Mark: 0

> *From: José*
> *To: Mike*
> *Thanks my friend. I'd like playing computer game. My everyday cost*

The question has not been attempted.

Paper 2   Listening

Part 1
1 A   **2** C   **3** C   **4** A   **5** B

Part 2
6 G   **7** C   **8** E   **9** F   **10** D

Part 3
11 B   **12** A   **13** C   **14** C   **15** B

Part 4
16 7/7th/seventh (September)   **17** Saturday   **18** JAGGARD   **19** (11) Park (Road)
20 photos/photograph(s)

Part 5
21 March   **22** (The) Visitor(s)('s)(s') (Centre)
23 2.15/14.15 (p.m.) (in the afternoon) / two fifteen / (a) quarter past two
24 (many different) toy(s)(and books)   **25** (£)4.25 / four pounds (and) twenty(-)five (p/pence)

Transcript

This is the Cambridge Key English Test. Paper 2: Listening. Test number one.
There are five parts to the test: Parts One, Two, Three, Four and Five.
We will now stop for a moment before we start the test. Please ask any questions
now because you must not speak during the test.

[pause]

PART 1   *Now look at the instructions for Part One.*

[pause]

You will hear five short conversations. You will hear each conversation twice.
There is one question for each conversation. For questions 1–5, put a tick under
the right answer.
Here is an example:
How many people were at the meeting?

Girl:	Were there many people at the meeting?
Boy:	About thirty.
Girl:	That's not many.
Boy:	No, but more than last time.

[pause]

The answer is thirty, so there is a tick in box C.
Now we are ready to start. Look at question one.

[pause]

Question 1   *One. How will Jill go to the football match?*

Man:	Are you going to drive to the football match, Jill?
Woman:	I was going to, but I think parking will be difficult.
Man:	That's what I thought. I'm going to walk, if you want to come with me.
Woman:	OK then – that's cheaper than the bus, and it's always late anyway!

[pause]

Now listen again.

[repeat]

[pause]

Question 2   *Two. Who's going to visit the woman?*

Woman:	My sister's son is coming to stay with me tomorrow.
Man:	Oh, that's nice. I met him a long time ago, when he was ten years old, didn't I?
Woman:	Well, he's a father now, you know. But he's not bringing the baby with him.
Man:	Oh, what a pity!

[pause]

Now listen again.

[repeat]

[pause]

Question 3   *Three. What will Ruby do tonight?*

Girl: Mum, Kate's just phoned. She wants me to go to the cinema this
               evening.
Woman: You can't go out, Ruby, if you haven't finished your school work.
Girl: But I have! And I've even cleaned my shoes.
Woman: That's all right then.

[pause]

Now listen again.

[repeat]

[pause]

Question 4   *Four. How much did the woman's desk cost?*

Man: I've just spent sixty pounds fifty on a new desk. Very expensive!
Woman: Well, I paid sixty-six pounds fifty for mine.
Man: I saw one for fifty-five pounds, but it wasn't very good.
Woman: A good desk costs more than fifty-five pounds.

[pause]

Now listen again.

[repeat]

[pause]

Question 5   *Five. Where is the man's watch?*

Man: I can't find my watch anywhere!
Woman: Did you take it off when you did the washing-up last night?
Man: I've looked in the kitchen and it's not there.
Woman: Here it is. You left it on the bath before you went to bed.

[pause]

Now listen again.

[repeat]

[pause]

This is the end of Part One.

[pause]

PART 2   *Now look at Part Two.*

[pause]

*Listen to Lena talking to a friend about some restaurants. What is the problem
with each one? For questions 6–10, write a letter, A–H, next to each restaurant.
You will hear the conversation twice.*

[pause]

Man: We've got to choose a restaurant for our class party next Saturday,
               Lena. What about the Rose Garden?
Woman: It'll be too cold, because all the tables are outside. I suppose Carla's
               Café is still closed.

Man:	It's open again now but it's not big enough for all of our class. What do you think about Pizza Place?
Woman:	The food's good, but they turn the lights so low, it's impossible to read the menu. What about the Curry House? The waiters are really friendly and everyone likes Indian food.
Man:	I phoned them yesterday – they're fully booked on Saturday so there won't be any tables free.
Woman:	Oh dear! I've just been to that new fish restaurant – Captain Crab. The music was so loud it was impossible to have a conversation.
Man:	We'll want to talk, so that's no good. I suppose there's the Carlton Hotel.
Woman:	Even a snack there costs a lot of money. We need a cheaper restaurant. Let's look in the newspaper . . .

[pause]

Now listen again.

[repeat]

[pause]

This is the end of Part Two.

[pause]

PART 3   *Now look at Part Three.*

[pause]

Listen to Helen talking to her friend Sam about being in a rock band. For questions 11–15, tick A, B or C. You will hear the conversation twice. Look at questions 11–15 now. You have 20 seconds.

[pause]

Now listen to the conversation.

Helen:	Sam, you know I sing in Nick's band?
Sam:	Mmm. He plays drums, doesn't he, Helen?
Helen:	Yes. Well, we need another guitar player. How about you?
Sam:	Sure!
Helen:	Nick wants to hear you play first. Are you free on Wednesday?
Sam:	Sorry. How about the next day or Friday?
Helen:	Let's say Thursday – Nick's busy on Fridays.
Sam:	Fine. Where and what time?
Helen:	Come to my flat at seven thirty and we can walk to Nick's. The band uses his dad's garage because his bedroom's too small.
Sam:	Should I bring anything? Food? Music?
Helen:	Nick's mum makes us sandwiches and I always bring CDs. A warm sweater's a good idea, because it gets cold.
Sam:	OK. When's the band's next concert? Aren't you playing at your brother's eighteenth birthday party?
Helen:	Yes, and the college has booked us for the Saturday before that. We want to play at the Starlight Club, but they're fully booked at the moment.
Sam:	Do you get paid for singing, Helen?

| Helen: | Of course – the band gets a hundred and ten pounds a night and we each have twenty-five pounds. Nick keeps ten pounds for things like advertisements. |
| Sam: | Great. |

[pause]

Now listen again.

[repeat]

[pause]

This is the end of Part Three.

[pause]

PART 4 *Now look at Part Four.*

[pause]

You will hear a man talking on the telephone about a party. Listen and complete questions 16–20. You will hear the conversation twice.

[pause]

Tony:	Hello, is that Sally?
Sally:	Yes?
Tony:	This is Tony Bassett. We were at Romford School together.
Sally:	Oh hello, Tony! I remember you well.
Tony:	There's going to be a party for the pupils in our year at Romford School.
Sally:	Oh – when will it be?
Tony:	Well, we started at that school on the fourth of September, but the party has to be on the seventh – almost exactly ten years later.
Sally:	That's a Saturday, isn't it? I know our first day at school was a Tuesday.
Tony:	That's right. Do you remember my sister, Margaret? It's at her house.
Sally:	Oh yes . . . she got married, didn't she?
Tony:	Yes. She's Margaret Jaggard now.
Sally:	Is that J A double G A R D?
Tony:	That's right. She lives in Park Road at number eleven, near the park entrance.
Sally:	That'll be easy to find. Can I bring something to eat or drink?
Tony:	There will be enough food, but everybody's going to bring some photos – we'll enjoy looking at them.
Sally:	I'll put the date in my diary.

[pause]

Now listen again.

[repeat]

[pause]

This is the end of Part Four.

[pause]

PART 5   *Now look at Part Five.*

[pause]

You will hear some information about a place called Sea World. Listen and complete questions 21–25. You will hear the information twice.

[pause]

Sea World is not open at the moment, but here is some information. We are open six days a week, from Tuesday to Sunday, from nine a.m. until five thirty p.m. Visitors are welcome from April to February, but we have to close in March for painting and repairs.

Every morning at eleven, there is a short film about the sea. Go to the Visitor Centre to watch this. The film is followed by a short talk about the different animals living in the sea.

The dolphin show begins at two fifteen every afternoon, but to make sure we can start on time, we ask everyone to be in their seats by two o'clock.

The shop at Sea World is open all day. Children will like the many different toys and books on sale there. There is also a café, where you can get drinks and snacks.

Adult tickets cost seven pounds and tickets for children are four pounds twenty-five. There are special prices for school groups.

Thank you for calling Sea World.

[pause]

Now listen again.

[repeat]

[pause]

This is the end of Part Five.

[pause]

You now have eight minutes to write your answers on the answer sheet.

Note: Teacher, stop the recording here and time eight minutes. Remind the students when there is **one** minute remaining.

[pause]

This is the end of the test.

Test 2 Key

Paper 1   Reading and Writing

Part 1

1 D   **2** H   **3** B   **4** A   **5** E

Part 2

6 A   **7** B   **8** A   **9** C   **10** A

Part 3

11 A   **12** A   **13** A   **14** C   **15** B
16 B   **17** E   **18** C   **19** H   **20** A

Part 4

21 B   **22** C   **23** B   **24** C   **25** A   **26** B   **27** A

Part 5

28 C   **29** C   **30** A   **31** C   **32** B   **33** B   **34** A   **35** B

Part 6

For questions 36–40, spelling must be correct.

36 library   **37** newspaper   **38** message   **39** board   **40** postcard

Part 7

For questions 41–50, ignore capitals / absence of capitals. Spelling must be correct.

41 with   **42** be/turn   **43** on/this/next   **44** have/'ve   **45** are
46 to   **47** of   **48** lot   **49** Would   **50** or

Part 8

For questions 51–55, spelling must be correct.

51 train   **52** Regent (Hotel)   **53** cathedral
54 (£)5.50 / five (pounds) (and) fifty (p/pence)   **55** castle

Part 9

Question 56

The three pieces of information that must be communicated are:

i   which sport the writer watched
ii   who they watched with
iii why they liked the competition.

Sample answer A

Mark: 5

> Dear Marey,
> How are you? I watched a competition horse riding in the evening. I watched this competition with my friend called Tome. I like horse riding because my father likes it too.
> With my best wishes,
> Mohamad

All three parts of the message are clearly communicated with only occasional grammatical errors.

Sample answer B

Mark: 4

> Hi Nick,
> I had watched fotball sport. I watched with my mother and sisters. I like to watched fotball sport because it had made my family happy, fun, and have more relationship.

All three parts of the message are communicated with some non-impeding errors in spelling and grammar.

Sample answer C

Mark: 3

> Hi Sylvie,
> Yesterday on the evening watched tennis on TV of course. It was very good game. I like this sport.
> the game was between A Thompson and E. Nisobet. Thompson played very good and she won.
> I hope that this game will be replay on TV.
> Marie

Two parts of the message are clearly communicated (the response does not address 'who you watched the competition with').

Sample answer D

Mark: 2

> Hi
> I like wathed football. My favorit tame is Sheffield W. and I am so happy
> when they wins with Sheffield untd. It is also very popular in sport in all
> the world.

Only two parts of the message are communicated (the response does not address
'who you watched the competition with'). The errors in expression may require
interpretation by the reader and impede communication.

Sample answer E

Mark: 1

> Dear Emma Which Sport do you watch. I wtacht' tennis. And hau did you
> wathe whith the competition with. And something its why did you like the
> competition love from Millie.

Only one part of the message is communicated. The response is very unclear.

Paper 2 Listening

Part 1

1 A   **2** C   **3** A   **4** A   **5** B

Part 2

6 F   **7** B   **8** G   **9** D   **10** A

Part 3

11 C   **12** A   **13** B   **14** C   **15** B

Part 4

16 Wednesday(s)/Wed(s).   **17** (£)8.50 (each)   **18** FERRET   **19** 7.45 / 19.45 /
(a) quarter to eight (p.m.) (in the evening)   **20** 136 / one three six / one hundred and thirty-six

Part 5

21 3/three (nights)   **22** FALKIRK (Hotel)   **23** golf   **24** Thursday   **25** 0208 66873

Transcript

PART 1   *Now look at the instructions for Part One.*

[pause]

You will hear five short conversations. You will hear each conversation twice.
There is one question for each conversation. For questions 1–5, put a tick under
the right answer.
Here is an example:
How many people were at the meeting?

Girl:	Were there many people at the meeting?
Boy:	About thirty.
Girl:	That's not many.
Boy:	No, but more than last time.

[pause]

The answer is thirty, so there is a tick in box C.
Now we are ready to start. Look at question one.

[pause]

Question 1   *One. Where will the man and woman meet?*

Man:	I'll see you outside the cinema at six o'clock.
Woman:	Why can't you meet me at the station? Or better still, the café? We're going to eat there before the film, aren't we?
Man:	Yes, but we need to be at the cinema at six to buy the tickets. Then we can go to the café.
Woman:	Oh OK.

[pause]

Now listen again.

[repeat]

[pause]

Question 2   *Two. What's the date of Emma's birthday party?*

Woman:	Are you going to Emma's twentieth birthday party in June?
Man:	Yes, I am. But it's in July actually.
Woman:	Oh yes, of course. The twenty-first, isn't it?
Man:	That's right. Her birthday is the day after mine. That's how I remember it.

[pause]

Now listen again.

[repeat]

[pause]

Question 3   *Three. Where is Norah's watch?*

Girl:	Have you seen my watch, Mum? I left it on the bookshelf.
Woman:	I think it's in the kitchen, Norah, on the table.
Girl:	That's your watch, Mum.
Woman:	Oh, then I'm wearing yours! Sorry, I thought it was mine.

[pause]

Now listen again.

[repeat]

[pause]

Question 4   *Four. How much is a ticket for tonight's match?*

Woman:	Are you going to the basketball match tonight?
Man:	How much are the tickets?
Woman:	Most weeks they're six pounds but it's a special price tonight – three pounds fifty – so do come.
Man:	Right. I've got ten pounds here, so that's OK.

[pause]

Now listen again.

[repeat]

[pause]

Question 5   *Five. Which is the boy's brother?*

Boy:	Look, there's my brother over there, talking to his friends.
Girl:	Oh, is he the one with dark hair?
Boy:	My brother's got blond hair.
Girl:	Oh yes, and he's got the same glasses as you. He looks nice.

[pause]

Now listen again.

[repeat]

[pause]

This is the end of Part One.

[pause]

PART 2   *Now look at Part Two.*

[pause]

Listen to Amy telling her father about her shopping trip. What did she and her friends buy? For questions 6–10, write a letter, A–H, next to each person. You will hear the conversation twice.

[pause]

Dad:	Did you spend all your money, Amy?
Amy:	No, Dad, but we all bought something. Look, I found the video I wanted.
Dad:	Great!

Amy:	We spent hours in the department store. Alison wants to take all her shoes on holiday, and her suitcase is too small. She bought a new one, but it took her ages!
Dad:	Then what did you do?
Amy:	We went with Helen to look at mobile phones. Her parents are getting her one for her birthday, so she bought a magazine that had information about all the different kinds to show them.
Dad:	That's a good idea. Did Lucy find a present for her mum's birthday?
Amy:	Yes, she looked at some beautiful shoes, but they were too expensive. But I think her mum will like the sweater she bought.
Dad:	Oh good. What did Kerry buy?
Amy:	A picture of our favourite band playing at a concert.
Dad:	Is that the band you saw with Jo?
Amy:	Yes. She got their new CD today. The music magazines say it's excellent.
Dad:	You must all be tired.

[pause]

Now listen again.

[repeat]

[pause]

This is the end of Part Two.

[pause]

PART 3   *Now look at Part Three.*

[pause]

Listen to Jamie talking to his mother about a flat. For questions 11–15, tick A, B or C. You will hear the conversation twice.
Look at questions 11–15 now. You have 20 seconds.

[pause]

Now listen to the conversation.

Jamie:	Hi, Mum! I've decided to move from my room at the university and into a flat with some friends.
Mum:	Is the flat near the university, Jamie?
Jamie:	About twenty minutes by bicycle and there are buses every half hour. But I'll walk through the park and have breakfast at a café there with my friends.
Mum:	Will the flat be quiet so you can study?
Jamie:	There's a shoe shop downstairs, but it's never busy, and there's not much traffic.
Mum:	Is it expensive?
Jamie:	Two hundred pounds a week, but there are five of us, so that's forty pounds each, which isn't bad.
Mum:	Good. Does the flat have a nice kitchen?
Jamie:	Well, the fridge is old and the cooker's a bit small, but that doesn't matter – we can't cook! Can I still use your washing machine, Mum, because there isn't one there?

Mum:	Of course. When will you move?
Jamie:	On Saturday.
Mum:	If you can wait until the next day, Dad and I will help you, so you're ready for classes on Monday.
Jamie:	OK. Thanks, Mum!

[pause]

Now listen again.

[repeat]

[pause]

This is the end of Part Three.

[pause]

PART 4   *Now look at Part Four.*

[pause]

You will hear a woman asking about tickets for the theatre. Listen and complete questions 16–20. You will hear the conversation twice.

[pause]

Man:	Queen's Theatre. Can I help you?
Woman:	Yes, do you have two tickets for this week's show? Saturday's best for me.
Man:	Well, all of the tickets have gone then, but we still have a few for Wednesday evening or Thursday afternoon.
Woman:	It'll have to be the evening. Have you got two near the front?
Man:	Let me see. I've got two seats, but they're near the back, I'm afraid.
Woman:	How much are they?
Man:	They're eight pounds fifty each.
Woman:	OK. I'll take them.
Man:	Then that'll be seventeen pounds altogether. Collect your tickets from the ticket office in Ferret Road. That's F E double R E T. The ticket office is open all day.
Woman:	OK. When does the show begin?
Man:	At seven forty-five in the evening. It lasts two and a half hours.
Woman:	That sounds fine. Can we get to the theatre by bus?
Man:	Yes, there's a bus stop just outside – take the one-three-six from the town centre. They go every eight to ten minutes.
Woman:	Thank you for your help.

[pause]

Now listen again.

[repeat]

[pause]

This is the end of Part Four.

[pause]

PART 5   *Now look at Part Five*

[pause]

You will hear some information about a competition to win a holiday. Listen and complete questions 21–25. You will hear the information twice.

[pause]

Here's some good news for all our listeners. Would you like to win a free holiday in Scotland? Yes? Well, the lucky winner of *The Travel Programme*'s holiday competition will win a three-night stay, for two people, in the wonderful Scottish countryside.

We have chosen a fine hotel for you. It's called the Falkirk – that's F A L K I R K, and it's an old castle in the mountains.

You won't have to pay for anything during your stay. The hotel has excellent food, and the competition winners can even use the beautiful hotel golf course when they are there.

All you have to do to win this great holiday is call *The Travel Programme* and answer the simple question we will ask you. Don't delay, because the competition closes at midnight on Thursday, and we'll tell you the name of the winner next Saturday. The number to call is oh-two-oh, eight-double-six-eight-seven-three.

Good luck, everyone. Now, here's the question for you . . .

[pause]

Now listen again.

[repeat]

[pause]

This is the end of Part Five.

[pause]

You now have eight minutes to write your answers on the answer sheet.

Note: Teacher, stop the recording here and time eight minutes. Remind the students when there is **one** minute remaining.

[pause]

This is the end of the test.

Test 3 Key

Paper 1   Reading and Writing

Part 1

1 G   **2** B   **3** F   **4** A   **5** E

Part 2

6 C   **7** A   **8** B   **9** A   **10** B

Part 3

11 A   **12** B   **13** C   **14** C   **15** A
16 H   **17** C   **18** A   **19** F   **20** E

Part 4

21 A   **22** C   **23** B   **24** C   **25** A   **26** B   **27** B

Part 5

28 A   **29** C   **30** C   **31** A   **32** B   **33** C   **34** A   **35** B

Part 6

For questions 36–40, spelling must be correct.
36 college   **37** museum   **38** station   **39** restaurant   **40** stadium

Part 7

For questions 41–50, ignore capitals / absence of capitals. Spelling must be correct.
41 am/'m   **42** was   **43** about   **44** would/should/'d   **45** or   **46** What
47 Have   **48** a   **49** next   **50** to

Part 8

For questions 51–55, spelling must be correct.
51 tennis   **52** Thursday   **53** 8(.00) (pm) (in the evening) / 20.00 (hours) / eight o'clock
54 3/three   **55** (£)30(.00) / thirty (pounds)

Part 9

Question 56
The three pieces of information that must be included are:

i   which items of clothing the writer bought
ii why they bought them
iii how much they cost.

Sample answer A

Mark: 5

> How are you?
> Yesterday I went shopping for clothes. I bought two trousers and one pair of shoes. I bought them because I have a birthday partie. Trousers cost each £20 and the pair of shoes it was free because direktor of this shop is my father.
> See you soon
> Željka

All three parts of the message are clearly communicated with only minor spelling errors.

Sample answer B

Mark: 4

> Hi Nick,
> YESTERDAY i WHERE iN SHOP TO BUY NEW CLOTHES. I BOUGHT A SWiMiNG COSTUME. i BOUGHT BECAUSE NEXT WEEK i AM GOiNG ON A SEESIDE. iT COSTED ABOUT £2.
> BYE
> TENA

All three parts of the message are communicated with some non-impeding errors in spelling and grammar.

Sample answer C

Mark: 3

> Hi Anna,
> Yesterday I went to do some shopping at 'Le Zagere' and I bought a new pairs of shoes and a black skirt because this evening I have a party.
> Élodie

Two parts of the message are clearly communicated (the response does not address how much the clothes cost).

Sample answer D

Mark: 2

> Dear John,
> Yesterday I was go to shopping. In a shopp I buy shows, dresses, touses, and clouthes.
> Someone are cheap and someone are expensive.
> Call me, please!
> Guillem.

Only two parts of the message are communicated (the response does not address how much the clothes cost). The errors in expression may require interpretation by the reader and impede communication.

Sample answer E

Mark: 1

> Hi Cornelio,
> Yesterday I went shopping. I went to new shopping centre. I bought many clothes: one T-shirt, two pairs of jeans, a trouser and a red pullover.
> Francesco

Only one part of the message is communicated.

Paper 2   Listening

Part 1

1 B   **2** A   **3** A   **4** C   **5** A

Part 2

6 G   **7** D   **8** B   **9** A   **10** H

Part 3

11 C   **12** A   **13** C   **14** B   **15** B

Part 4

16 (at) 6.00 / 6/six o'clock (in the morning)/(a.m.)   **17** (the) school(s) / (school) children/students
18 (£)7.50 / seven pounds (and) fifty (p/pence)   **19** 9(th) (of) March / 9.3/09.03/3.9
20 FOWLER

Part 5

21 (The Elephant) Doctor   **22** ARGYLL   **23** (Saturday) (the) 30(th)/thirtieth (of) (July)
24 4/four (tickets) (per family)   **25** (a) book (about the film)

Transcript

This is the Cambridge Key English Test. Paper 2: Listening. Test number three.
There are five parts to the test: Parts One, Two, Three, Four and Five.
We will now stop for a moment before we start the test. Please ask any questions
now because you must not speak during the test.

[pause]

PART 1   *Now look at the instructions for Part One.*

[pause]

You will hear five short conversations. You will hear each conversation twice.
There is one question for each conversation. For questions 1–5, put a tick under
the right answer.
Here is an example:
How many people were at the meeting?

Girl:	Were there many people at the meeting?
Boy:	About thirty.
Girl:	That's not many.
Boy:	No, but more than last time.

[pause]

The answer is thirty, so there is a tick in box C.
Now we are ready to start. Look at question one.

[pause]

Question 1   *One. Which boy is Peter?*

Girl:	You've got a lot of photographs of your family. Who's this one of?
Boy:	They're my cousins.
Girl:	So which one is Peter, the one you're always talking about? This one here?
Boy:	That's right. He's standing in the middle because the other two weren't speaking to each other that day.

[pause]

Now listen again.

[repeat]

[pause]

Question 2   *Two. Which day will they go to the cinema?*

Boy:	I'd love to see that film about the boy who learns to fly. I think I'll go on Thursday. Do you want to come too?
Girl:	I can't that night – I'm going to play tennis with Dave. How about Tuesday . . . or if not, Wednesday?
Boy:	Tuesday night is fine. I can't on Wednesday. I'll see you outside the cinema at seven then.
Girl:	OK!

[pause]

Now listen again.

[repeat]

[pause]

Question 3   *Three. What are they going to do on Saturday?*

Boy: Come to the beach on Saturday.

Girl: I'd like to, but I must finish some work for the History lesson on Monday.

Boy: Haven't you heard? There are no classes on Monday because of the football match.

Girl: Oh great! I'll go with you then. My next History lesson isn't until Friday.

[pause]

Now listen again.

[repeat]

[pause]

Question 4   *Four. Where does Paul live?*

Boy: I'm going to Paul's house to watch a video. He's living in our street now.

Woman: In the house that was for sale? Number thirty-two?

Boy: The one next to it, thirty-three. And Kevin from school is coming to live here too, at number thirty-one.

Woman: All your friends in the same street . . . I'll never see you!

[pause]

Now listen again.

[repeat]

[pause]

Question 5   *Five. Where are they going to put the computer?*

Boy: Can I have the new computer in my bedroom, Mum?

Woman: It's for all the family to use, so we really need it downstairs. What about putting it in the kitchen?

Boy: It gets very hot in there. The living room is nicer.

Woman: Well, it's noisy when the television is on, but we can try it there.

[pause]

Now listen again.

[repeat]

[pause]

This is the end of Part One.

[pause]

PART 2   *Now look at Part Two.*

[pause]

Listen to Janet talking to her friend about a party. What did each person wear? For questions 6–10, write a letter, A–H, next to each person. You will hear the conversation twice.

[pause]

Janet:	Hi, Sue. How are you feeling?
Sue:	A bit better, thanks, Janet. Tell me about Emma's birthday party at the weekend. What did you wear?
Janet:	My long skirt, as usual. Emma looked great. One of her presents was a sweater with gold flowers on the front, and she wore that.
Sue:	I suppose Mike was there in that suit he always wears.
Janet:	He was in jeans – but they were black and he looked great.
Sue:	Was he with Michelle? She wanted to wear my white jacket, but it was too small.
Janet:	She had on a blue Chinese dress, and Rachel was wearing blue too.
Sue:	I know, the blouse with the silver buttons – I've seen her in it before. It looks lovely with her silver shoes.
Janet:	Jason came straight from work, so he'd still got on that T-shirt he wears at the restaurant. Even in winter he never wears a sweater.
Sue:	Well, the girls all had nice clothes anyway. Let's hope I can come to the next party.

[pause]

Now listen again.

[repeat]

[pause]

This is the end of Part Two.

[pause]

PART 3   *Now look at Part Three.*

[pause]

Listen to Zak talking to Maria about his sports bag. For questions 11–15, tick A, B or C. You will hear the conversation twice.
Look at questions 11–15 now. You have 20 seconds.

[pause]

Now listen to the conversation.

Maria:	Hi, Zak, this is Maria. I got a message about your sports bag but I didn't understand it.
Zak:	Thanks for phoning, Maria. I'm still in hospital, so can you get my sports bag from school? It's blue, not black and white like my school bag.
Maria:	OK. What size is it?
Zak:	It's quite large and it's a good bag. I only bought it a few weeks ago, but it needs a wash!

Maria:	Where is it?
Zak:	Well, I had it on the sports field with me, but Tim took it to the classroom after my accident. I left it there when they brought me to hospital.
Maria:	Is there anything inside it?
Zak:	Only my school uniform. I'm wearing my watch, and I never carry money in it.
Maria:	OK. Shall I bring it to the hospital after school?
Zak:	I'm going home this afternoon. Can you take it there this evening? I'll need it for tomorrow morning.
Maria:	Sure. How did you hurt yourself anyway?
Zak:	It was after football. We were running back to the changing rooms when I fell.
Maria:	Oh dear!

[pause]

Now listen again.

[repeat]

[pause]

This is the end of Part Three.

[pause]

PART 4   *Now look at Part Four.*

[pause]

You will hear a man asking for some information about a swimming pool. Listen and complete questions 16–20. You will hear the conversation twice.

[pause]

Man:	Hello, I'd like some information, please. Is the swimming pool open every day?
Woman:	Not on Monday, I'm afraid.
Man:	I like to swim before breakfast. What time do you open?
Woman:	We open the doors at six o'clock for the first swim of the day, the 'early morning swim', we call it. That's the best time to come, because after seven it gets very busy.
Man:	I see.
Woman:	And don't come between nine thirty and twelve thirty because schools use the pool then. It's closed to everyone else.
Man:	OK. Do you have lessons? I want to learn to swim better.
Woman:	Yes, every afternoon. It's seven pounds fifty a lesson or seventy pounds if you pay for ten.
Man:	OK. When does the next course begin?
Woman:	Let me see . . . it's on the ninth of March. Would you like to start then?
Man:	Yes please. What's the teacher's name?
Woman:	It's Roy Fowler. That's F O W L E R. He's an excellent teacher.
Man:	Well, thank you very much. My name's . . .

[pause]

Now listen again.

[repeat]

[pause]

This is the end of Part Four.

[pause]

PART 5   *Now look at Part Five.*

[pause]

You will hear some information about free cinema tickets. Listen and complete questions 21–25. You will hear the information twice.

[pause]

Here is some good news! We have some free cinema tickets for you. They usually cost five pounds.

   They are for a film called *The Elephant Doctor*. It's about a man who works in a zoo and looks after the animals when they aren't well. It's a great film for all the family.

   All you have to do to get your free tickets is send your name and address on a postcard to Radio South-West in Bristol. The address is twenty-seven Argyll Road – that's A R G Y double L.

   Send your postcard soon! Make sure it arrives before next Saturday, that's the thirtieth of July. All the postcards will go into a bag and we will choose the twenty-five winners then.

   We have one hundred tickets to give away, but I'm afraid we can only give four tickets to each family because lots of people will want them. And we will send everybody who writes to us a book. This is about the film and has pictures of the actors and the animals in it. So send us that postcard now!

[pause]

Now listen again.

[repeat]

[pause]

This is the end of Part Five.

[pause]

You now have eight minutes to write your answers on the answer sheet.

Note: Teacher, stop the recording here and time eight minutes. Remind the students when there is **one** minute remaining.

[pause]

This is the end of the test.

Test 4 Key

Paper 1   Reading and Writing

Part 1
1 B   2 F   3 D   4 A   5 G

Part 2
6 C   7 A   8 C   9 B   10 A

Part 3
11 B   12 A   13 B   14 C   15 B
16 A   17 E   18 B   19 G   20 C

Part 4
21 B   22 A   23 A   24 C   25 A   26 B   27 C

Part 5
28 C   29 A   30 C   31 A   32 B   33 B   34 A   35 A

Part 6
For questions 36–40, spelling must be correct.
36 farmer   37 mechanic   38 journalist   39 waiter   40 photographer

Part 7
For questions 41–50, ignore capitals / absence of capitals. Spelling must be correct.
41 at/in   42 called/named   43 where   44 am/'m   45 than   46 the
47 of   48 him/studying/school   49 a   50 to

Part 8
For questions 51–55, spelling must be correct.
51 (next) Tue/Tues/Tuesday   52 (she) (wanted) Italian (food)
53 (at) 7.30 (p.m.) / 19.30 / seven thirty / half past seven   54 18/eighteen
55 (£)20(.00) / twenty (pounds)

Part 9

Question 56
The three pieces of information that must be communicated are:

i   the time they will meet
ii   how they will get to the sports centre
iii   what the writer should wear.

Sample answer A

Mark: 5

> Dear Sarah,
> I'm happy to hear you would like to play tennis this evening. We should
> come 4 o'clock this evening to my house. We can go by my car to the
> sport centre. You should wear a shorts and a T-shirt.
> Bye.
> Sachini

All three parts of the message are clearly communicated with only occasional grammatical errors.

Sample answer B

Mark: 4

> Hello Sarah, come to seven o'clock at my house and we can after take my
> car for the sport centre. And come whiff a t-shirt and short. OK?

All three parts of the message are communicated with some awkwardness of expression.

Sample answer C

Mark: 3

> Dear Mario,
> How are you? I write you because I want to tell you that we are going to
> meet at 7pm in my house. We are going to get to the spot centre wiht
> the help of my parents. Call me.
> Bye. Fabio

Two parts of the message are clearly communicated (the response does not address what to wear) with only minor spelling errors.

Sample answer D

Mark: 2

> *Dear Sarah,*
> *This after noon we well meet to ply tennis. About 5. pm i well meat you at*
> *my house. We well going by my car.*
> *Yours,*
> *Taher*

Only two parts of the message are communicated (the response does not address what to wear). The errors in expression may require patience and interpretation by the reader and impede communication.

Sample answer E

Mark: 0

> THANK FOR YOUR LATER. I MET IN YOUR HOUSE LAST WEEK. I WENT TO
> THE SPORTS.

The question has not been attempted.

Paper 2   Listening

Part 1

1 B   **2** A   **3** C   **4** A   **5** B

Part 2

6 E   **7** B   **8** H   **9** G   **10** F

Part 3

11 A   **12** B   **13** C   **14** B   **15** C

Part 4

16 River(s)   **17** (Martin) COOPER   **18** 123–127   **19** fish   **20** Friday

Part 5

21 5(th) (July) / 5/(0)7 / 7/5   **22** (and) drum(s)
23 (0)9.15 / nine fifteen / (a) quarter past nine (a.m.)
24 (£)3.25 / three pounds (and) twenty-five (p/pence)   **25** 217 3881

Transcript

This is the Cambridge Key English Test. Paper 2: Listening. Test number four.
There are five parts to the test: Parts One, Two, Three, Four and Five.
We will now stop for a moment before we start the test. Please ask any questions
now because you must not speak during the test.

[pause]

PART 1   *Now look at the instructions for Part One.*

[pause]

You will hear five short conversations. You will hear each conversation twice.
There is one question for each conversation. For questions 1–5, put a tick under
the right answer.
Here is an example:
How many people were at the meeting?

Girl:	Were there many people at the meeting?
Boy:	About thirty.
Girl:	That's not many.
Boy:	No, but more than last time.

[pause]

The answer is thirty, so there is a tick in box C.
Now we are ready to start. Look at question one.

[pause]

Question 1   *One. What are the boys going to do?*

Boy:	Let's go fishing. You never want to play football unless there's a lot of people. And it's too hot to play tennis, isn't it?
Friend:	I don't think so. If we play in the park, we can go and get a drink in the café there afterwards.
Boy:	Well, all right . . . but I don't want to play for long.
Friend:	OK. It'll be fun, you'll see, and fishing is boring anyway.

[pause]

Now listen again.

[repeat]

[pause]

Question 2   *Two. Which tent does the girl choose?*

Man:	This tent's very nice – it's big enough to stand up in.
Girl:	But I need one that I can carry.
Man:	This round one's for three people, and not too heavy. And this one here is for two people, so it's even lighter.
Girl:	Oh, that'll be best. I'm travelling alone but the extra space will be nice.

[pause]

Now listen again.

[repeat]

[pause]

Question 3   *Three. Which one is Ruth's bike?*

Girl: I'm taking your bike to the library, Ruth. Is that all right?

Friend: Fine. You can use the bag on the back to put your books in.

Girl: Yours has got a water bottle too, hasn't it? I don't want to take the wrong one.

Friend: That's right.

[pause]

Now listen again.

[repeat]

[pause]

Question 4   *Four. What does Sarah's dad do?*

Boy: Are your mum and dad both doctors, Sarah? I saw them in the hospital together yesterday.

Girl: Only my mum is. My dad was a cook, but he works for the hospital now. He drives an ambulance.

Boy: That's nice for them, to work in the same place.

Girl: Yes, my dad is much happier now.

[pause]

Now listen again.

[repeat]

[pause]

Question 5   *Five. Which picture is the woman asking about?*

Woman: You have some lovely pictures for sale. Can you tell me who painted the one in your window? It's very good.

Man: The oil painting of the Swiss mountains?

Woman: That's beautiful, but I meant the one below it.

Man: Oh, the summer flowers – that's by George Anderson. Look, there's a picture of him here in this art magazine.

[pause]

Now listen again.

[repeat]

[pause]

This is the end of Part One.

[pause]

PART 2   *Now look at Part Two.*

[pause]

Listen to Kerri talking to a friend about her new room. Where do they decide to put her things? For questions 6–10, write a letter, A–H, next to each thing. You will hear the conversation twice.

[pause]

Boy:	I really like your new room, Kerri. It's so big.
Kerri:	I know. There's even space for my computer. I'm going to put it on the desk.
Boy:	Great idea! Shall I put these books on the shelf?
Kerri:	They're dictionaries. Leave them on the floor near the desk – I use them all the time.
Boy:	OK. Now, what about your plant? It'll look nice on this table.
Kerri:	Hmm, it should be by the window. Can you put it on this big cupboard? Be careful – it's heavy!
Boy:	OK.
Kerri:	I'd like the lamp near my bed, but there's no room.
Boy:	Well, let's move this small cupboard, and then it can go on the table, like this.
Kerri:	Great! And throw me that pillow, please. It should be on the sofa – I don't want it on the bed.
Boy:	Fine. And why have you still got this old toy bear, Kerri?
Kerri:	I don't know. It's always been on my bed. It can go on the shelf now. Is that everything?
Boy:	Yes.

[pause]

Now listen again.

[repeat]

[pause]

This is the end of Part Two.

[pause]

PART 3   *Now look at Part Three.*

[pause]

Listen to Jim talking to Sarah about things to take on holiday. For questions 11–15, tick A, B or C. You will hear the conversation twice.
Look at questions 11–15 now. You have 20 seconds.

[pause]

Now listen to the conversation.

Sarah:	Hi, Jim. I like your walking shoes. I haven't seen any like them in England before.
Jim:	They're Italian, Sarah. I got them for my holiday in Austria last month.
Sarah:	I need some like them, because I'm going to go there too.
Jim:	Not many shops sell them. I got mine at the market, but they may have some at the new supermarket.
Sarah:	How much were they?
Jim:	I think they usually cost sixty-eight pounds, but mine were only forty-eight – so I paid twenty pounds less. I was really pleased.
Sarah:	I'll get some this afternoon. Is there anything else special I should take?
Jim:	Well, pack a hat, because the sun can be strong in the mountains. I took a sweater and a jacket, but I never needed them.

Sarah:	Anything else?
Jim:	Take lots of T-shirts, one for each day you're going to go walking.
Sarah:	That's five days of my week's holiday. And what about taking a phone?
Jim:	Well, there'll be one in your hotel, if you want to call home. But take yours, because then you can call someone if you get lost in the mountains.
Sarah:	Thanks, Jim.

[pause]

Now listen again.

[repeat]

[pause]

This is the end of Part Three.

[pause]

PART 4   *Now look at Part Four.*

[pause]

You will hear Sally asking a friend about some homework. Listen and complete questions 16–20. You will hear the conversation twice.

[pause]

Sally:	Hello, Richard. I wasn't at school today because I was ill. Can you tell me what our Biology homework is?
Richard:	Yes, Sally. In class, we talked about animals that live in water. For homework, we have to read a book about them. The book's called *Rivers*. It's in the school library.
Sally:	OK. Who is it by?
Richard:	Let me see . . . it's by Martin Cooper.
Sally:	Is that C double O P E R?
Richard:	That's right. You'll find the books on the third shelf on the Biology bookshelf. We have to look at part seven, pages a hundred and twenty-three to a hundred and twenty-seven.
Sally:	OK. That's not very much. What is it about?
Richard:	That part's all about fish. It's quite interesting. Mrs Knight says we're going to study lakes next week.
Sally:	Oh, right. Do we have to read these pages for the lesson on Monday?
Richard:	We have until Friday to do it.
Sally:	Oh good. I'll go to the library on Thursday. Thanks, Richard. See you tomorrow.

[pause]

Now listen again.

[repeat]

[pause]

This is the end of Part Four.

[pause]

PART 5   *Now look at Part Five.*

[pause]

You will hear some information on the radio about a summer music school. Listen and complete questions 21–25. You will hear the information twice.

[pause]

We are pleased to tell you that this year there will be a summer music school at the Arts Centre. Classes at the summer music school will begin on the fifth of July and will go on until the thirtieth.

The school is open to young people between the ages of eight and seventeen. There will be classes in piano and guitar . . . and, have you ever wanted to play the drums? Well, you can learn at the summer school. The teachers are all really excellent.

There will be classes every morning from Monday to Friday, beginning at nine fifteen and finishing at eleven forty-five. It doesn't matter if you have never had music lessons before. Beginners are welcome. Students will only have to pay three pounds twenty-five a day, or fifteen pounds for a week.

For more information about the classes, or to book a place, phone the Arts Centre on two-one-seven, three-double-eight-one.

So, that's the summer music school. A great place to play music and make new friends.

[pause]

Now listen again.

[repeat]

[pause]

This is the end of Part Five.

[pause]

You now have eight minutes to write your answers on the answer sheet.

Note: Teacher, stop the recording here and time eight minutes. Remind the students when there is **one** minute remaining.

[pause]

This is the end of the test.

Sample answer sheet – Reading and Writing (Sheet 1)

 UNIVERSITY *of* CAMBRIDGE
ESOL Examinations

S A M P L E

Candidate Name
If not already printed, write name
in CAPITALS and complete the
Candidate No. grid (in pencil).

Candidate Signature -

Examination Title

Centre

Supervisor:

If the candidate is ABSENT or has WITHDRAWN shade here ▭

Centre No.

Candidate No.

Examination Details

KET Paper 1 Reading and Writing Candidate Answer Sheet

Instructions

Use a PENCIL (B or HB).
Rub out any answer you want to change with an eraser.

For **Parts 1, 2, 3, 4** and **5**:
Mark ONE letter for each question.
For example, if you think **C** is the right answer to the
question, mark your answer sheet like this:

 0 A B C

Part 1		Part 2		Part 3			
1	A B C D E F G H	6	A B C	11	A B C	16	A B C D E F G H
2	A B C D E F G H	7	A B C	12	A B C	17	A B C D E F G H
3	A B C D E F G H	8	A B C	13	A B C	18	A B C D E F G H
4	A B C D E F G H	9	A B C	14	A B C	19	A B C D E F G H
5	A B C D E F G H	10	A B C	15	A B C	20	A B C D E F G H

Part 4		Part 5	
21	A B C	28	A B C
22	A B C	29	A B C
23	A B C	30	A B C
24	A B C	31	A B C
25	A B C	32	A B C
26	A B C	33	A B C
27	A B C	34	A B C
		35	A B C

Turn over for
Parts 6 - 9 →

Sample answer sheet – Reading and Writing (Sheet 2)

For **Parts 6, 7 and 8:**

Write your answers in the spaces next to the numbers (36 to 55) like this:

0	example ✏️

Part 6		Do not write here
36		1 36 0
37		1 37 0
38		1 38 0
39		1 39 0
40		1 40 0

Part 7		Do not write here
41		1 41 0
42		1 42 0
43		1 43 0
44		1 44 0
45		1 45 0
46		1 46 0
47		1 47 0
48		1 48 0
49		1 49 0
50		1 50 0

Part 8		Do not write here
51		1 51 0
52		1 52 0
53		1 53 0
54		1 54 0
55		1 55 0

Part 9 (Question 56): Write your answer below.

Do not write below (Examiner use only)
0   1   2   3   4   5

Sample answer sheet – Listening

UNIVERSITY of CAMBRIDGE
ESOL Examinations

S A M P L E

Candidate Name
If not already printed, write name
in CAPITALS and complete the
Candidate No. grid (in pencil).

Candidate Signature

Examination Title

Centre

Supervisor:
If the candidate is ABSENT or has WITHDRAWN shade here ⬚

Centre No.

Candidate No.

Examination Details

0	0	0	0
1	1	1	1
2	2	2	2
3	3	3	3
4	4	4	4
5	5	5	5
6	6	6	6
7	7	7	7
8	8	8	8
9	9	9	9

KET Paper 2 Listening Candidate Answer Sheet

Instructions

Use a PENCIL (B or HB).

Rub out any answer you want to change with an eraser.

For **Parts 1, 2** and **3:**
Mark ONE letter for each question.
For example, if you think **C** is the right answer to the
question, mark your answer sheet like this:

| 0 | A B C |

Part 1

1	A B C
2	A B C
3	A B C
4	A B C
5	A B C

Part 2

6	A B C D E F G H
7	A B C D E F G H
8	A B C D E F G H
9	A B C D E F G H
10	A B C D E F G H

Part 3

11	A B C
12	A B C
13	A B C
14	A B C
15	A B C

For **Parts 4** and **5:**
Write your answers in the spaces next to the
numbers (16 to 25) like this:

| 0 | example |

Part 4

		Do not write here
16		1 16 0
17		1 17 0
18		1 18 0
19		1 19 0
20		1 20 0

Part 5

		Do not write here
21		1 21 0
22		1 22 0
23		1 23 0
24		1 24 0
25		1 25 0